The Way to Rainbow Mountain

Poems by

Susan Deer Cloud

The Way to Rainbow Mountain

Copyright © 2019 by Susan Deer Cloud

Cover design by Kristen Torralba

Photo of Rainbow Mountain in Peru by Susan Deer Cloud

Library of Congress Control Number: 2019948390

ISBN: 978-0-9600931-0-6

Published by Shabda Press
Pasadena, CA 91107
www.shabdapress.com

Acknowledgements

With sincere gratitude to the editors and publishers who included some of these poems in *The Way to Rainbow Mountain* in the following literary journals and anthologies: *Art Against Hate*; *Local News: Poetry About Small Towns*; *Mountains Piled Upon Mountains, Appalachian Nature Writing in the Anthropocene*; *Anacua Literary Arts Journal*; *Cape Cod Poetry Review*; *K'in*; *South Florida Poetry Journal*; *Paterson Literary Review*.

Abiding appreciation for my editor/publisher, Teresa Mei Chuc, dear honorable poet —and for esteemed writers Stephen Page, Amy Krout-Horn, and Gabriel Horn who gave this book such beautiful and generous blurbs.

Forever thanks to the doctors, nurses, technicians, aids, receptionists, piano man, etc., who helped me defy cancer.

The Poet's Preface

In May 2017 I was diagnosed with breast cancer, and in a sense this book, *The Way to Rainbow Mountain*, spirals out from when my doctor told me the biopsy results – to both before that sad day and following it. The cancer had been caught at an early stage so, lucky me, I would merely require a lumpectomy and three weeks of external beam radiation treatments with a "boost" of a few more treatments. Next I could begin taking tiny white Anastrozole pills for five years to keep estrogen at bay, because breast cancer absolutely dotes on estrogen. I doubt that this will come as a surprise to any reader of discerning sensitivity and empathy, but getting cancer is never lucky and anyone who says so is just another bullshitter denying suffering people's reality. I am only fortunate in the sense that cancer can be ever so much worse, as I witnessed when my maternal grandmother plummeted through a spring to autumn nightmare of brain cancer (dead at 60) and my mother spent two unspeakable years dying of metastasized breast cancer (dead at 59). I am only fortunate inasmuch as I have learned all over again how loving, kind, supportive and understanding human beings can be to someone who is dealing with a disease that can kill them. I am also ironically lucky in the sense that getting cancer confirmed for me what certain people were made of, including those who didn't show their faces until they thought the cancer coast was clear or totally dropped out of sight. And how could I not notice that I was diagnosed with breast cancer not long after Donald Trump was inaugurated as the 45th President of the United States, when hatred metastasized in my beloved country? The absurd symbolism and surreal metaphors of that most unfortunate conjunction of my cancer with the new Crazy proved to be almost overwhelming. No wonder during the 2017 summer of surgery and radiation treatments I increasingly watched murder mysteries on PBS!

Not to worry. I did not end up murdering anybody. Being more of a detective, I sought to solve the puzzle of how to shine on in an affirmation of bravery, creativity, exuberance, beauty, tenderness, caring, and love. I chose to "keep going" as my mother, her sisters, and my grandmother often said we must do despite our losses and sorrows. And I certainly did keep going, all the way to South America with my roving companion in November 2017, not even three months after my last radiation treatment. Moreover, we returned to South America in October 2018, eventually traveling to Peru's sacred Machu Picchu and even more enthralling Rainbow Mountain. Yet during all those wanderings, I felt always that I carried my first home with me, the Catskill Mountains, as well as my "blood family" and "spirit family" back on what I call Turtle Island. Before the cancer, my companion and I made a road trip to the Maritime Provinces of Canada, a mirroring of Chile, Argentina, Bolivia, and Peru in terms of unique wild mesmerizing beauty, danger, and intensity that steals beneath one's skin in an unshakable way. That far north trip and those extreme south treks in Latin America comprise Part II of *The Way to Rainbow Mountain*, whereas Part I focuses on *this* America, the starting point for my story interweaving with myriad other people's stories. Lengthy rambles in foreign lands turned into kaleidoscopic transformations of the heart/mind; new experiences alchemized into poetry. Ultimately, I hope this book conveys to any gentle reader the importance of being as brave as possible so that the human spirit can do what it was intended to do – sprout wings and sing as the great Chilean poet/artist/musician, Violeta Parra, sang – *Gracias a la Vida*, "Thanks to life."

Susan Deer Cloud, late summer 2019

The Way to Rainbow Mountain is dedicated to

my artistic cousin, Kristin Noelle Krupp, who I value greatly,
and her children, Little Lena and Liam –

my great nieces & nephews: Brodie, Danny, Ramsey, Lily, Ella, Evie
& Amelia Hauptfleisch and Aurora Bryant–

all those who stood by me after I was diagnosed with breast cancer,
especially Erelene, Michelle, Danny the elder, Lynn and John –

every human being of shining spirit who has touched me deeply
and taught me profoundly during my long wild ecstatic rovings –

Contents

PART I

"One must endure without losing tenderness" (Che Guevara)

It Is There I Will Take You To

(for Genevieve Collura whose poet's light danced on too soon)

It is there I will take you to – places
only I know about, far from cities and politics –
Catskill hideaways beneath evergreens
or hardwoods leafing out in dreamcatcher light.

It is May I shall take you to, after bare November
and deer season's slain does and bucks, after
the holidays and mad buying and all of us
trying to have our nostalgia dinners

with family and jolly friends like the ones
on Christmas cards starred with glitter.
Long after the cold comes and snow
metastasizes across mountains

the same as cancer blows through the barrens
of your bones, I will bring you to where
the daffodils and hyacinths flame forth,
the forget-me-nots and spring beauties –

and robins singing once more near mosses
soft enough to rest upon in the reborn sun.
By then winter's surgery, chemo and radiation
will be like faded memories of ice storms,

of pain and dark night prayers.
It is there to where spirits never die
I will lead you, where my ancestors lived
and had children and hope. I will show you

their graves and the way we still speak
to each other from our two worlds.
You will see where my ancestress
the medicine woman had her cabin

and drowned in Mongaup Creek.
Dear sister, young friend, in that valley
we shall kick off our battered boots
and dance barefoot and flamboyant again.

Bone Song

When I read about that high limestone cave
looking out on the Anuy River's sinuous silver
parting Siberia's summer mountains, when
I saw the photographs showing the bones
found there, an old bear femur flute song
shrilled through my 21st century bones
resonating to what the scientists found
among the scattered shards –

90,000 year old female bone fragment
whose mitochondrial DNA whispered
her mother was Neanderthal, whose
other DNA murmured her father was Denisovan.

Did that female have some sense of what I call
the Great Mystery? Did she create a language?
Did that *being* whisper poetry or begin to sing
when sun welcomed her wakening each morning
at cave opening, smiling at rays conjuring up
star sparkles on a river where later she would
finger-fish and swim nakedly in the pure waters.

Little dreaming bone rescued from the cave's
sedimentary layers, could you feel your sun again
when scientists brought you up for air
after all those unsmiling centuries? And
what my intuition clamors to know
since my DNA holds lineage both Neanderthal
and Denisovan, and my mitochondrial migrations
include ancient grandmothers dwelling in Siberia –

Am I descended from you, dear Hybrid?
Are you somehow the reason why I am sparked
to write poems and lilt stories with epicanthic eyelids
around northern campfires? Are you why I wear
this hair long and have felt it as residual fur
whenever making love? Are you the key
to why even as I migrate into old age, I still go
skinny dipping in a starry river?

Tracking Panther

Not to kill does she track the Eastern Cougar
called Panther in her homeland Catskills –
where foothills crescendo in swells to high
Slide, Cornell, and the Wittenberg.
Not to hunt it down as bounty hunters
stalked her Indian ancestors, but
just to see it – greet glowing eyes
with glowing eyes. Not to skin it

that way settlers did, holding up
thick pelt, bragging about the glory
of it until the wild cat of death got
their tongues – nor slay feline beauty
like they destroyed Natives they renamed
"savages," slicing off an ear, a nose,
a strip of skin, a "Redskin," easier
to lug in for bounty than an entire body.

Not to murder does she track Panther,
ghost-walker of her Manitou Mountains –
Indian-named Onteora, Land in the Sky.
If she beheld the great cat
glistening through mist, shying low
through hemlocks and balsam firs,
she would meet it with those glints
in her eyes old-timers exclaimed

matched the gold flames in Panther's
eyes. She would flash back to girlhood
dawn she heard cougar screams behind
the house, sobs still in her heart.
Not to prove anything, not to murder,
not to brag. Just to be able to say
Woodlands Indians are not extinct
but with Panther shape-shift into mist.

Let Me Tell You About My Indian Grandfather

Let me tell you about my Indian grandfather,
how he was dragged off to an orphanage
after his mother crashed through the ice
while ice-fishing, fought her way out
only to die of pneumonia. Let me tell you
what it was like for that nine-year-old boy,
the times he ran away until he was able
to stay in the mountains where eventually
he died of a heart attack, young, the way
so many in our family die. Let me speak
his freedom, for instance the high noon
he borrowed that horse the color of a unicorn
belonging to the stone mason he worked for,
racing its white beauty up and down Main Street,
blazing through a gauntlet of small town faces
while shooting his pistol off in the spring air –
a raven-haired, high cheek-boned Indian
on a tear because another young man tried
to steal my grandmother. Let me tell you
how he galloped home, stood glaring
with a cigarette on his front porch,
blowing blue smoke rings until the cops
squealed in with sirens and tried to play cowboys
with his wild Indian, threatening to arrest him –
how he lifted his pistol and shot
bullets around their polished shoes.
"Dance," he laughed, "dance, or I'll shoot

9

your toes off!" They started dancing
while the horse the color of a unicorn
snorted, rearing up in its own dance.
"Now waltz on out of here and don't
threaten me again!" They stumbled
to their car and Grandpa resumed blowing
sacred circles and enjoying the lilacs
and forget-me-nots all around. Let me
tell you about my Indian grandfather
who spoke one word, "Mother," before
his great freedom-loving heart gave out.

Clingmans Dome Before Thanksgiving

(for John Gunther)

Lovers at their beginning –
driving from friends' house in Mashulaville, Mississippi,
to Smoky Mountains

all night through Deep South sleeps,
Spanish moss hanging like lynched ghosts
in Confederate-gray mists

until entering in

they make it in time to dash up
steep dirt path to see dawn
like Cherokee shawl of rose and gold

weaving light around blue peaks
and human limbs shivering
child-small in that immense place.

Driving along steep mountainsides
and down deep valley roads, snake

twists, perilous drops, at each turn
beauty re-birthing the sacred
not far from where Cherokees

tend their fire in a secret woods
on the Tennessee side of boundless blues.

Meandering up and up
to ice-enshrined Clingmans Dome,
stepping out on park's highest peak,

wind piercing flesh to the awed bone,

beneath feet white fog sea, peaks
purple bruises when mists tear free,
sun sears through –
frozen trees, frost-furred wildflowers,
and lovers lit to glistening.

Opening Night

(for Rane Arroyo, in memoriam)

Opening night in Woodstock, New York.
Of course, the films made of your bestselling
memoir, *Naked Like a Constellation*,
and mine, *Borscht Belt Indian*,
could have opened anywhere. We
considered Sundance, the Cannes
of Indie films, but for such wild poets
accustomed to parallel universes
even Sundance is too establishment.

You once jokingly emailed me
in the days you didn't really think
the movie of you could happen – and we
were being silly about the possible stories
of our impossible lives – "We can go
in matching dresses," after I wrote
your memoir was destined to be a film
whose gala opening I fully expected you
to invite me to.

Yes, you who I call pen pal, the boy
who was supposed to be there when I
was an Indian girl in 1960s Catskills,
the grown professor who bills himself
as Gay Puerto Rican Poet from the Midwest,
O Amigo, O Rane, O Byron of Toledo, Ohio,
who shimmers in shirts of orange flame
shielding a heart of fire,

I never doubted this October day
poised between Libra and Scorpio
would come. Once you mentioned
the lonely little boy now so stunned
he grew up to know talented people
like me. Me? The lonely little girl
stunned as any butterfly on a highway
of windows? But you – gifted

and brilliant brother who understands
about being hit – you never shut
me out, never let my wings tear against
the glass of cruelty and too fast life.
Ah, you and I, literati metamorphosed

to glitterati, in matching red dresses
with scarlet shoes like Dorothy's
("No moccasins, dear Deer,"
you stomped your foot down) –

naturally you appear more sexy (How do
you gay guys do it? Give us some tips!).
Longtime partner at your side, you both
bedazzle. I invited all my former lovers, at least
a trillion (ha ha, you couldn't invite yours!)
They want to bask in my green eyes again,
feel the light of a Star swaying arm
in arm with another Star. We sashay
down Tinker Street through crowds
tossing roses before us,

dreamer wannabes cheering at
gorgeous us gazing up at sky stars
like celestial dresses matching our blaze.
You and I smile, wave, as if we've known
no gutters, only how to be divas of our own
intimations of immortality played by
Eric Bana and Jessica Alba. We float
towards the double feature waiting within,
as in the long hot summers of childhood matinees,

of handsome cowboys and Indians seducing us
to love them in Technicolor. At the Tinker Street
Cinema entrance, you hug me knowingly.
Sí, I remember your early days of doubt,
also my struggle to write my life when I am
but a weave of secrets in a pattern of pipe dreams.
I recall why you said you needed to do this –
not for you but for all the violated angels
who don't know how to write about themselves.

"It's my honor," you said, "to give them
what they deserve." And swept inside
by a tornado of laughter on Tinker Street,
I remember why I had to do this. We toss
our Oscar Wilde wigs high in the air,
click together our sparkly heels –
lonely little Puerto Rican boy, lonely
little mountain girl – at last
their beautiful heartbreak up in lights.

Nasty Woman Blues

Woke up this morning, election over, snow
coming down, hail to the Tweeter-in-Chief.
Thanksgiving near, Northeast buried
by a storm from the Atlantic and a storm
from the West and anybody's guess
as to what might blow in next.

Woke up at dawn, wondered if I should
yawn back to sleep and hibernate with bears,
except the Pussy Grabber-elect made
this nasty woman recall FDR's
"The only thing we have to fear
is fear itself," so I kissed my old man
dreaming he was a wild child again,

stroked his silvery hair soft as mists
shrouding mountains outside our door,
swung my brave feet to cold floor,
the nasty woman blues greeting me
in an America that doesn't feel
like "home, sweet home" anymore.

Shivered out of bed this morning,
snow pelting down, deer and birds
disappeared, when was there ever
a place for me here, born a "part
Indian" girl to a poverty land,

a cat-eyed outsider, exotic and sexy,
smart and poetic, talk about being
called "nasty," I was light years ahead
of the white girls whose feminist forbears
were inspired by my Iroquois ancestresses.

Sisters, I know what you get when
you're uppity, I've been pussy-grabbed,
slapped black-eyed, my hair yanked so hard
I hurt forever from whiplash. My words
have been censored by those on the Right
and those on the Left, Indians and non-Indians.

Branded a "witch" and a "bitch," this nasty poet
could write a saga about stormy weather.
Woke up this morning in a country full of turkeys,
hunters in the woods, snow strangling sound
and me coming down with the nasty woman blues,
trying to sing what's left to be thankful for.

Mountain Women's March,
January 21, 2017

January morning Sun ascended
into a little spring in January, bloom
of rose light in sky bluer than your Blues –
you rising with Catskill dawn
that day of the Women's March in D.C.
and other big cities girdling

the globe, staying in mountains
of Indian ancestresses who grew
star-silent during centuries
of being hounded and shamed.
No pink pussy hat for you. No shouting
outrage to the crowd, no defiance

delivered in the F-words of celebrities
who got chauffeured back to safe mansions
when the excitement died and workers
came to sweep garbage off the dark streets.
Since 1968 you had attended marches,
cradled candles in countless vigils,

and, of course, always voted –
now angry and disheartened,
knowing who refused to vote in a way
that would have given the U.S. a better
President. That day when Sun raised
her bright fist past high noon

you drove your sister and a Swedish friend
out of your one red light town occupied
more by ghosts than people in a county
of foreclosed houses, zombie faces, kids
dying of smack and pills, doomed babies,
where Trump signs were winter's weeds –

three women meandering through
mountains and valleys to ancient Delaware,
talking, smiling, hoping, laughing
as those in mountain matriarchies do,
eating lunch together at the River Café,
delighting in sun sparkles flashing

down fast currents on which
Indians once canoed from village
to village. And later traveling
secret woodland roads where doe eyes
watched you aging sisters flame by
in a spring that could not last.

Even in Winter Witches Fly

Two weeks since January 20, 2017, inauguration
of the pussy grabber whose name I try not to mention,
instead recall our Iroquois way of saying "I don't know
that person" when a human being lies, swaggers, values
gold more than soul and shows disrespect to women
and all of Mother Earth. Just two weeks and me

shivering and hurrying home from Post Office
in town I grew up in and returned to in 2013,
a writer in her sixties who when the time arrived
wished to die where so many of her people's bones
dreamed in Catskill graves, where native roots
reached deep, town she fled at seventeen because

of violent gossips who hated anyone different,
who thought me weird for loving literature, art
and foreign films, folk music and peace/love,
for writing poems instead of being a cheerleader
believing football and basketball stars were gods
and females must remain virgins until marriage

when a pumped up player would metamorphose
into swan or bull, break the prize such boys jeered
was cheerleader cherry. After the inauguration
tears kept surprising my eyes, until I scolded myself
out loud, "You need to stop, maybe it won't be as bad
as you fear, don't let this overshadow your life."

But then that early February of no thaw when
I heard teenage boys snickering behind me traipsing
down snowy sidewalk in long purple coat and trailing
Labrador scarf whose colors made me think of
northern lights when I first saw it hanging on a store
wall in Maritime Canada. In my small hometown

with its little minds that drove anyone unique away
or to suicide, I whirled around to see who was laughing
in tones I knew too well, spotted the mockers scurrying
across Main Street, the biggest thug wannabe yelling
"Where's your broom?" before sprinting far ahead,
four faceless cowards, turned backs in dark coats,

unlike me with silver hair streaming down, coat hem
painting spells in drifts left over from the last storm,
full moon face shocked back to all the taunts of a lifetime,
stomach sick and me almost crying despite myself. "Is this
what it will be now?" I wondered. "Human pack dogs
attacking old women and other Others as witches again?"

Eventually, I the poet, old hippie-Indian, different one,
started smiling because those boys did get my power right,
smiles turning to laughter at how they fled from this witch
wild and wise in her crone clothes, kicking up snow diamonds
with each step while knowing how to curse a person if it came
to that, greeting my blue broom when I made it home.

Mountaintops, Appalachia

Took her decades to realize why she hated
driving on Pennsylvania's Route 81
past Honesdale, Scranton, Wilkes Barre
and other towns whose inhabitants
looked as if they ate dirt and their eyes
were made of dark mica.
"The coal, the coal," it shocked
her brain like an eclipse one day
when she couldn't escape taking 81
on her way south, which meant she
couldn't avoid the trucks, constant
construction, and strangely shaped
hills left along the highway after
the coal mines closed.
All that digging up of Mother Earth,
that long rape of the land, the endless lie
of mountains really an ancient plateau
worn down to what can pass for beauty.
A slash of loneliness between
the bereft earth and ghosts who spent
decades digging for coal, buried
when alive, buried again when dead.
And then there was West Virginia
southern sister to her Catskills,
both filled with people a crazy quilt
of nationalities with Indian mixed in,
born to be free-spirited. But hunger
can drive even the most defiant to be

low, to go underground and shovel coal,
just takes children crying, cold in rags.
Then the mines there started to close
and the CEOs in shiny shoes
and polished offices in faraway cities
chose to blow the mountaintops off,
more coal higher up once the machines
took over and rich men were happy to blast
apart all that Appalachian beauty.
She had seen her share of mountains
dynamited so roads could go through.
How would she feel if men came north
and stole away the mountaintops,
what would it do to the trout streams
and the people who were singers
and storytellers and spoke in soft voices?
She had known the tattered dreamers
who left for the cities and never returned.
She signed the petitions protesting
the removal of mountaintops, called
representatives and senators, all
the usual that seemed to end up
where wool socks and mittens go.
For a while it even looked hopeful
until the 45th President barged in,
his view towards Mother Earth
the same as his view towards women.
Poor poet that she was, she understood
desperation and depression. Nothing
against those people down there
in that sister place like the Catskills
only farther south. She knew how

it took the top of her heart off
when men, women, and children
shuffled by with heads hung low,
looking like their eyes were dark mica
and they'd been forced to eat shit.

Water Protectors

Out there – North Dakota water protectors,
Standing Rock Sioux making a stand against
Big Oil snaking a pipeline through
sacred land and under the Missouri,

from everywhere Indigenous
and non-Indigenous people chanting
"Save the water, save the water." As usual,
cops came with tear gas, guns, rubber bullets –

but, unlike in the past, videos of the assaults
ricocheted across the Internet. Now
everyone can flinch at what a rubber bullet
does to a boy warrior's face, or mace

to a girl dancer's eyes. Here –
Catskill elder lays her body in red poncho
on a beach of stones by the Beaverkill,
beloved river whose unpolluted

waters heal her whenever
she floats downstream between
mountains like guardians on two sides.
Remembering Wounded Knee Uprising –

1973, younger self like the Indians
in those videos, visionaries crying from
fierce sweet hearts, believing if something
is as right as keeping Earth's water pure

the dreamers will win. There
in North Dakota – the beautiful young
and the beautiful old, and a baby just born.
Here her autumn arms hugging

medicine bag a Cherokee man gave her
after she survived to her fiftieth birthday,
Bear Clan symbols with beading he learned
from a great grandma at Wounded Knee –

inside turquoise skin her medicine bundle,
mystery wrapped in soft blue cloth. Here
distant voices in water running fast as buffalo,
on shore a wild prayer.

The Great Revolutionary

The Great Revolutionary was a philosophy major
at a private university, a suburban boy
whose parents paid for his "pad," food, tuition,
threatened to disown him when they learned
he was shacking up with a flower child who ran away
from her state college to make revolution with him.
The Great Revolutionary used to sweet talk the rebel
from a poor mountain family into writing his papers,
a revolutionary act so he wouldn't get drafted and sent
to Nam. Five years later another Great Revolutionary
snickered to the wild child her old lover married a rich girl,
became a life insurance salesman on Long Island.
She went hungry, returned to college, wrote her own papers,
graduated summa cum laude, became a published poet
adept at hiding scars behind a perpetual smile.

The Great Revolutionary invented "free love"
raised to orgasmic heights in the 1960s when
The Pill made the scene. He balled hippie chicks
with no fear of a shotgun wedding, and if
they bore his children he helped them dig
how marriage equates women's oppression.
The Great Revolutionary was a professor
who taught master courses on D.H. Lawrence,
meeting with coeds for special office sessions
involving a phallic symbol full of Jack Daniels
inside his desk. The once straight-laced prof
dropped acid, metamorphosed into a groovy guru

quoting Alan Watts, abandoned his oft pregnant
faculty wife for students who "gave head"
in all ways, including brilliant repartee
until dawn. Happily, when university girls got
knocked up they had abortions, no big deal.

The Great Revolutionary was a chameleon,
expert at sniffing out the Zeitgeist, whining
Bob Dylan's "The Times They Are A Changin'"
long after his idealism putrefied into a petrified lie.
The Great Revolutionary embraced every
feminist notion *du jour*, especially men not paying
for women's dinners or opening their doors.
Secretly he masturbated to all those bra-less breasts,
that way nipples at Women's Lib rallies stood erect.
The Cheap Revolutionary praised Black Power
then Red Power, danced at powwows, did sweats,
wore beads. When he tried peyote and saw he was
Crazy Horse's reincarnation, he proposed marriage
to a Sioux beauty who reminded him of his first crush,
a hick hippie chick who ran away with a college boy
who stole the country of her body and soul, a poet-dreamer
with medicine enough to take back her uninsured life.

The Great Revolutionary still jacking off.

The Streets of Liberty Are Empty

Mid-July Tuesday following that Sunday when ICE barged
into the rooms of fear, seeking men, women, children, babies
lacking green cards and citizenship papers – terror ordered
by the clown President who pretends he's a Christian –
mass arrests mocking his lie of a sabbath. As usual,
evangelicals and other hypocrites roared their approval
in Fox News' ear-hurting arrogance, racists conveniently
forgetting their ancestors were illegal immigrants, including
slavers and invaders committing genocide, just ask any Indian.

July 2019 in Liberty, New York, in searing Catskills
once dubbed the Borscht Belt when immigrant Jews
sought refuge in hotels they built in these mountains
because those who claimed to love Jesus barred them
and Black people and Hispanics from staying at their
hotels reeking of bleach. As for the Indians, they were
contemplating suicide on reservations or lying low,
even passing for White, in the wilder places, including
these forests and rivers we call Onteora, Land in the Sky.

On that day Richard, friend whose skin might be
considered a coat of many colors, White, Black and Red
all over just like old time news (get it?), rode into town
on his rounds of delivering beer for the People who needed
cooling down, for those thirsting for joy in an era of hate.
As he later told Karin, his Swedish wife the blond Socialist
with eyes of radical blue fire, something felt different,
eerie, on the streets of Liberty, and then the shock of it –
the once hopping tourist town was now unpopulated

except for those we "bleeding hearts," we "snowflakes,"
try not to call "white trash" taking over the emptiness,
phantoms milling around zombie-like in a heroin haze,
ghosts on fentanyl flirting with death, panhandlers
stumbling gaunt and toothless from years of meth, eyes
black holes. No Mexicans, no one from Latin America,
talking, laughing, and dancing freely as they used to do,
nothing hinting they existed except their closed restaurants
and apartment windows locked shut in ninety degrees heat.

America, your haters are getting the "Great" they screamed for –
the streets of Liberty are empty.

At the Blue Robin Diner, Binghamton, NY

Lingering at the Blue Robin, Upper Court Street.
Hiked there for greasy spoon eggs over easy, short
stack of blueberry pancakes, coffee more like
wannabe coffee (but still God to me). Figured
I'd walk along summer solstice road bordered
by railroad tracks and first wild chicory blown
wilder by spray painted freight trains, reward
myself with what the waitresses call "eats" while
waiting for my old Toyota, Purple Wampum Pony,
to be inspected by my favorite mechanic. Yearning
for the days of unlicensed horses galloping across
a freer past, I wince at young waitress addressing me
as "Ma'am." I quip, "Please don't call me ma'am,
Goddess will do." Her pretty pout makes clear
she'd like to call me "Bitch," but before I'm done
eating pancakes and the blueberries that taste like
BP oil globs, we are lamenting the Gulf of Florida
from where she has returned. On wall next to
a huge smudged window hangs photographs,
an eagle and owl peering down. They remind me
of my visit with that Cherokee man last week,
how one night after drinking Pinot Noir and watching
"The Lives of Others" his poet eyes surprised me –
in living room's soft lights showing the softer
far in light of the Indian man who can peer
as an owl or eagle into the eyes of any woman
who bears that same Native light. I remember

his gifting me with a feathering of joy before
he headed west, of our rambling together
in my Catskill Mountains, seeing an eagle
soaring and spiraling as two Native people do
when for once they don't need to explain.
If you are Indian you will appreciate what I mean
about explaining. And you will understand
why we laughed and sounded like the rivers
and sparkles of light on the rapids, despite
knowing how it is to feel like a dry creek bed
strewn with storm-broken branches. Yes,
lingering in the Blue Robin – an invisible
eagle feather and owl feather drifting down
and "getting it on" in the blues of my heart
which early this morning beat like a bird's
heart when I wandered barefooted into
the rose-walled guestroom where the Cherokee
had slept and I curled up on the bed,
wrapping red satin sheet around naked skin,
hearing again how he said, "You make me
emotional." I wanted to be with his tears
like first starlight, Big Bang topaz and amber
glinting along the ledges of high cheekbones.
Fuck, I wanted to be wherever people really feel.
In the Blue Robin Diner sipping the dregs
of now cold coffee, watching the people
of the other world of diners everywhere,
smiling soft as that one June evening's lights,
realizing I would never have to explain to that
Cherokee my cocooning the butterfly remnants
of me in the guest bed's chrysalis of sheet.
Waitress drops the blue check like a fluttering

wing. I leave a five star restaurant tip, goddess-me
having toiled as a waitress in a hotel snack bar
when I was bittersweet sixteen, also because I am
watched over by Owl and Eagle and a bird-eyed man
whose hands feathered mine with kindness.

Indian Hills

Snow-haired woman yawns
    five stories high on bed in Indian Hills,
1930s building giving a nod to Natives
    who centuries ago lived in Inwood Park,

peers awed through tall
    windows inviting in New York lights
near and far, Henry Hudson Bridge
    twinkling in swoops evoking Catskills

she hails from, of stars
    and ancestors, the Ongwe:Howeh,
the Shining People. Early April,
    warm enough that her lover raises

windows, spring air floating
    across naked bodies, mates growing
old yet holding hands like children
    about to skip somewhere for daffodils

in an endless spring. Winging
    asleep she marvels over birds singing
even though day had already flown
    into its own Dreamtime –

strange to hear birds chirping at midnight.
    In some dark hour she wakes to spring rain,
and still the birds' serenade. Breeze now wind,
    wild rhapsody casting a spell over Indian Hills,

hand in lover's hand 'til sunrise,
    mists silvering Manahatta and ghosts who she
in her half-sleep believes shape-shifted
    from vanished Indians to immortal birds.

People I Have Fallen In Love With On The A-Train

A man with snow cloud hair, face bowed
into a book while all the other riders toy
with cell phones or stare at that point only
New Yorkers can find in subway train air,
disappearing through its black hole.
But not this man with features half-hidden
hinting at the life lived in his tweed suit
frayed at its cuffs. Man from another time,
more like the epoch of reading I grew up in.
Hands intricacies of blue veins, elegant fans
propping up the book my squinting eyes
finally make out to be Charles Dickens'
A Christmas Carol. Man whose mouth
moves as if he is tasting sugar plums,
savoring each word on Christmas Eve 2016,
whose lips I wish I could kiss into a story
before he slips off the A-Train to become
another ghost of Christmas past.

Korean-American couple
who manage to lift their baby stroller
onto the train, their baby girl tucked
under a pink quilt color of azaleas
in a spring many moons away.
The baby's cheeks plump and silken
as petals, eyes peering up at me
from beneath epicanthic eyelids

like the eyelids I had when a child.
So in love, this husband and wife,
the way I remember my mother and father
in their twenties, flowered with a flame
and tenderness able to create a universe
wherever they went. The man conjuring
up Korean poet once my lover,
how we longed to be a holy family
but were too split by age. Daughter
gurgling her happy language among
legs swaying to the rocking of the A-Train,
Papa lifting her laughing into the song
of his and Mama's encircling arms.

First the voice, "Please help me,
please help me," floating down
from A-Train car's far end where
African-American boys are giggling.
Next a tall black man like a king in rags
strides past their mockery, holding out
his right hand, chanting his anguish
to passengers who earlier had been
warned by a recorded announcement
not to give money to people panhandling.
Melodious the man's voice yet containing
all the broken-heartedness and desperation
that ever was, back to our original mother
who dreamed us in Northern Africa.
Hand pressing money quick into his
passing hand, most hands clenched,
faces looking away. Next to me
a café au lait teenager drops change

sounding like jingle bells. Handsomer
than Duke Ellington riding to Sugar Hill,
the panhandler king collapses in seat
opposite us after I add a silent dollar,
him with the eyes of Jesus filling
with tears on Christmas Eve.

It isn't the young woman who first
draws my eyes, but the ad she sits
under, colors blaring ADORE ME
and *It's not about V-Day, it's all
about #Meday*, behind the words
a model of indeterminate race
modeling lacy black bra and panties,
lips receptive with laughter. Who feels
joy like that universal female anymore?
Certainly not the woman with the sad
Chinese features below, black-haired
in black-rimmed glasses, black jeans,
black quilted jacket and black sneakers,
huge black knapsack propped on her knees,
wisps of hair straggling free from strict
ponytail, darkening her high cheekbones.
Face turned in a gaze towards an invisible
place or person I shall never know. All
I know is the lost year my own countenance
glimmered tragic as hers, not expecting
adoration or a reason to smile ever again,
not even an A-train to take me somewhere.

Living Out Your Dreams
in New Orleans

When you curled corpse-like
  near hospital window
you couldn't turn your eyes to,
  neck bones broken
by metastasized breast cancer,
  could you have imagined
this New Orleans' night, Ma,
  on that autumn high noon, 1985,
day I kept vigil by bedside
  in Sayre, PA, chemo dripping
silent tortures into your veins,
  tears dripping pain
into your still exquisite face –
  Could you have foreseen
your daughter same age
  as you when you lay dying,
imagine her habitation of
  You live out my dreams,
I wasn't able to,
  now they've broken my spirit –
when I cried *No, that isn't true,*
  your spirit remains,
and you spoke no more?
  So this sublime night of me
and poet friends flown
  South for mid-March poetry tour,
dancing more than walking

through Vieux Carré,
Louisiana breeze blowing
       our hair into jazz wildness
until we gust into Gold Mine Saloon –
       Patrick, Vincent, Marlon, Paulette and me
the Mine's featured readers
       already high from drinking
at the Napoleon, and after
       we read and open mic poets let it rip-
roar in that man-made hip cave
       hosting 14-karat lights and dark matters
of lust, hurricanes, manic-depressions,
       we spill out to corner
of St. Peter and Dauphine
              (*Hey, y'all, we're goin' to the Night Hawk*)
and I sprouting wings, Ma,
                     headed for another funky bar
and life's real saints playing
       sax, piano and super strings –

Would you have smiled once more
       if you could have seen this future me
scrambling up on ridged bed
       of Sweet William Lavender's
big ol' poet pickup truck,
       squeezing between Marlon and Patrick
while Paulette, my first NOLA anarchist,
       smiles all *laissez les bon temps roulez*
next to Lavender blazing away
       from illegal parking spot
('*Cause cops here don't bother
       with trivialities since Katrina*),

40

our trinity enthroned on Wild Bill's over sized
        highly symbolic tool box
(*Hey, where's Vincent?*
        Dunno, man, probably on a vision quest
for a Cuban cigar to smoke
        where every man's a king) –
Bewitching hour of poets laughing like kids
        tumbling into each others' bodies
each time Bill's White Buffalo of a truck lurches
        into another street, then *Damn!* –
Patrick chanting *Cop, cop, cop,*
        me shouting while still laughing,
Patrick, didn't you learn anything
        in the 'Sixties? Don't look at a cop,
don't blink at a cop, don't think cop, don't speak cop –
        and big mouth stops saying *cop*, certainly
not *pig*, just gets on his Irish *mad eye*
        as police car melts
into the Quarter's neon streamings
        while Marlon's bearded countenance
blooms into his saki beatitude
        of a Zen Buddhist grin –
This, Ma, *all this*, so tell me,
        in the City of the Dead
are you whole and beautiful again?
        Can you find a window
you can turn gray eyes to
        and peer through at daughter
you abandoned to many nights
        of abandonment – girl you seduced
raven-haired husband for
        one New Year's Eve because

you *wanted a daughter,*
and you got your passion child
beyond what you ever bargained for?

Oh, Ma, thank you, Sweet Mama,
for this ride with rhyming ecstatics,
the enraptured, the holy dreamers
whose neon-lit faces I will not forget
as I don't forget yours –
flying through New Orleans'
starry neon night eternally hung
over from Mardi Gras,
honoring your dreams, Ma,
strange blessings in swirling
lights and colors like beads
tossed to the flashing mysteries,
starship and fuckship
of Wild Bill's truck riffing
with ghosts of Fats, Satchmo, King Oliver
and sad mad glad jazz
of my life, your life, our Storyville –

Coffee Girl

You perched on an antique chair
in pale dining room of a Southern belle
in her late eighties. Baton Rouge
sunshine flashed across your freckled
fingers cradling big blue coffee mug,
its hue making you think of the Blues
you listened to in New Orleans
the night before, of neon-lit
singers with skin like evening sky
and eyes the keepers of the first
stars seeding what became
our blue planet and explosion
of seven billion human skins.

"Y'all sure do like your coffee,"
the coiffed belle sipped her tea.
"I love my coffee," I agreed,
praying the fragile chair would hold
under me. "I love everything
about it, the taste, rich color,
steam that kisses my face
and the daily ritual of sitting down
with my cup o' Joe and memories
of drinking coffee with others,
talking and laughing away our Blues."

"Never drink it," the old belle chimed.
"Yearned to when I was a gal
visiting my grandma, watching her
and her friends drinking expresso.
I wanted to be grown up like them.
One day I grew brave enough to ask
 if I could have a cup of coffee, too.
'Why, you sure can,' she grinned,
'only when nice white girls drink coffee
it turns their skin black. Y'all want
to be a lil' pickaninny, honey?' Of course
I didn't want to become a *you know*."

She hastened to say she was glad things
had changed in the South, shrugged
"We didn't know any better back then."
I kept sipping my coffee mixed with cream,
wondering how she really felt about
having me, a Blackfoot au lait, in her mansion,
remembering my girlhood friend the other kids
taunted with the name "pickaninny" and worse.
Clementine, wherever you disappeared to,
I raise my blue mug of poetry to your beauty black.

Calcifications

In the mammogram room the word
sounded prosaic – calcifications
the specialist said. But I read faces,
am an expert on tone, so a next word
did not surprise me – biopsy.

Then the silence that seemed so long
before the doctor filled in my blank,
hastened to say that ninety percent
of calcifications are negative.
I wanted to be a believer,

I who had tried for sixty six years
to laugh off my mother's lamentation
There's a curse on our family.
But how could I when she had been
diagnosed with breast cancer,

died after twenty moons at fifty nine?
Other words metastasized in my mind –
I'm not going to live, am I? –
The death of a beautiful woman,
most powerful theme in literature –

O ye of little faith –

Mid-May, in not too many days
the biopsy. Before they pushed
the long slow needle in, glimpse
of calcifications on computer screen –
white, tiny, like faraway stars

or snow crystals twinkling right before
a windshield wiper hurls them away.
How pretty the Sky World of that breast.
Had past lovers sensed that star shine
all the way back to the Big Bang?

Did the darlings who long ago
caressed that breast over my heart
feel delicate crystals alight
like life's dice in their hands,
the gamble of spirit in matter?

Not Long After Sunrise

I wake and walk to sliding door
across bedroom's east wall
to watch the rainy dawn, glimpse
doe and newborn fawn slip
in the silence between raindrops
into spring bushes whose flowers
have begun to fall, white scatterings
like rice tossed at a wedding
from long ago when all was hopeful.

For weeks I have been searching
for the doe who comes every year
in this way, for the fawn she brings,
as though it is always the same mother
who seeks out the stream silvering
behind ancient lacy spruces
good for shelter, leading
that fawn whose spots blaze
in first light and the mists

fading when rain gives way
to sun spreading red wings over
Catskill sky. How often have I
stood thus enthralled, me, the doe,
the fawn? Only this sunrise I sway
at open door with cancer crouched
in my left breast, remembering
my mother who had breast cancer,
beautiful as deer, disappeared.

Penny Candy Pentimento

(for Benjamin Halpern)

Your way through photographs, mine through poems.
You the long ago boy whose parents' store beckoned
not far from our town library, made me as happy
as signing out books. Shadows, soft-lit, hinted
at lacy blouses, bikinis, shiny shoes, vivid lipsticks
and other marvels, but mostly I noticed candies
for just a penny each behind glass counters –
and the great awed eyes of a Jewish child
doubling as a dance of light, sometimes invisible,
other times shying into sight. These fall days
when I saunter up Main Street towards the library,
I still see the old store beneath new German bakery,
after all these decades feel lucky pennies jingling
in my dress pockets – a dreamy poor girl poised
like a prayer before a cornucopia of candies until
I finally asked your mother and father to please
give me hot balls, red licorice, nonpareils, bubblegum,
root beer barrels, wax lips, and chocolate coins wrapped
in gold. I didn't know they were Walter and Belle –
back then grownups were Mr., Mrs. or Miss.
I only knew your name, Benjamin, an evocation
of old Jacob's beautiful surprise son. How polite
we mountain people in the 1960s – the manna
of my choosing making me feel rich and dignified
when I sashayed out the door into the day's weather.
But not until I skipped to the free library and got

new books did I place a candy on my tongue, joining
its sweetness with reading once I arrived home.
Your way, Benjamin, through photographs'
black and white pentimento, each image a street,
a door, a room leading into another and another,
or a face leaping out then leaping into past faces
and story upon story. My path through each poem's
black and white palimpsest, metaphors, similes,
symbols, allusions trekking across a white page
that is street that is snow that is wildflower that is sky,
fragments of former people and places glinting through.
"Goddammit," you cried after I was treated for breast cancer,
"you had better not die!" Thank you for that, thank you.
I won't, and you won't – the bookworm girl who learned
to live forever through poetry, the penny candy boy
whose photography rhymes with eternity.

What They No Longer
Saw in the Catskills

When her grandma was born following the fin de siècle
the white-tailed deer were gone, although the family
dwelled on a mountain called White Roe. Disappeared

the old growth forest, chopped down for firewood,
furniture, cabins. Hemlocks that once cast ghostly
green-blue across endless swells and rounded horizons

had been stripped for tannin to make beaver hats
for city gentlemen who preferred fashion to trees.
Passenger pigeons were extinct, but sometimes

someone spotted a black bear in a blackberry patch.
By the time she came along in 1950, so had DDT.
She never saw a great blue heron or bald eagle,

although the deer had been reintroduced, venison
a part of their wild meat meals along with trout,
rabbit, and ruffed grouse the natives called

partridge. A Dutch elm kept her company
outside her upstairs bedroom window,
branches bowing low like ballerinas

she dreamed of seeing. The disease hit
and her father had to chainsaw down
her dying friend. That winter they stared

into the fireplace, elm wood crumbling
in flames. The State deemed the Catskill panther
extinct, even though she heard one scream

behind the house. The Government lied
that non-treaty Indians were like all the other lives
disappeared, but her People were merely

incognito, blending in with the quiet places.
Once grown, she ran away to the big cities
and neon lights to see those ballerinas

and be with urban men. Four decades later
she made her way back along with the blue herons
and bald eagles – and, she prayed, the panthers.

When Fox First Came, 50th Anniversary of the Summer of Love

When Fox first came she had no name for it –
she a poor Catskill Indian girl working
in a Jewish hotel at a gravel road's dead end,
sixteen year old waitress hustling to make
tips to save for college. When Fox

showed up, most people she served
food and drinks had no name for her invisible
in white waitress dress, hand-me-down
from aunt who worked in a diner in her teens.
When Fox made the scene

it was 1967, beginning of the end
of the Borscht Belt's heyday,
start of what journalists dubbed
the Summer of Love. She toiled late
into the nights against child labor laws,

especially after weekend shows
when the hotel's guests rushed down
to the snack bar, demanding egg creams,
ice-cream sodas, fudge sundaes –
she and other waitresses dashing

back and forth to please the wives
in sequined dresses and the husbands
who pinched and slapped their asses

whenever their women wouldn't see.
No one spoke of "sexual harassment,"

it was just something one kept mute about
to earn bigger tips. When Fox appeared
it was a Sunday between shifts.
She wandered into the forest past the hotel,
sat down beneath a beechnut tree,

weary from working until 3 AM,
feet aching so she slid off sneakers
to feel the cool shade as balm to her skin.
When Fox arrived she had fallen far
into a sleep like death. Maybe it was

such dreamless stillness that lured
the creature blushing close to the body
curled and virginal on soft green ferns –
and the fern green eyes that finally fluttered
open to eyes flashing wonder
into hers. She gazed at what glowed
like starlight all the way from the universe's
Big Bang, she was with the Great Mystery,
invisibility and pain ebbing away
into the receiving Earth. When

the word FOX blazed across her brain,
firing it back into human consciousness,
the creature who stayed by her when she slept
trotted off like the dream she was too tired to have.
She brushed twigs and dirt off flesh that shone

redder than before, shying back through
fragrant woods to the hotel, to the birth
of the Summer of Love, to the beautiful
boys of that time who suddenly could not
keep away from her in those wild moons

when free love became the mantra
of the young growing hair long and soft
as mountain flowers, those "hippies"
the fearful called "animals" – and she
the "Foxy Lady" Jimi Hendrix wrote about.

Heathcliff's Moor

This late summer mist floats me
back to that December I was fourteen,
to Christmas Eve day when my parents
were still alive and they and my brothers
and little sister and I traipsed up
a back mountain road in winter fog.
How like silvery wraiths my family,
glimmering the way tinsel glowed
on our Christmas tree. I loved them so.

I had just devoured Emily Brontë's
Wuthering Heights. The Catskills' ghostly air
evoked the South Pennines' high wild moor
where Catherine and Heathcliff loved –
"He's more myself than I am. Whatever
our souls are made of, his and mine are the same."
How I wanted such love, a dark boy others scoffed
was a "Gypsy," more myself than I. But any
passerby would have merely glimpsed

a virgin in holly-green dress and coat
nearly invisible in the mute fog
made musical with laughing voices. Unseen
I dreamed of flying to the moorland
where Heathcliff and Catherine roved.
This late summer mist transports me
back to four springs ago when my lover
took me to that very place, when sun
rose to 10 AM yet still couldn't pierce

mists shrouding fields and paths,
lambs and shaggy cattle ambling curious
to fences, and then the faded wood sign
pointing to Brontë Falls. All hilly moss,
lichen-painted rocks and long emerald grass
it shone beside the unbridled stream, and we
tramped along the creek until we reached
the waterfall. To think our soaked hiking shoes
inhabited the phantom footsteps of the three sisters,

of those Brontë girls whose holy fire blazed
like that May sun dispelling the fairy mist at last.
On to Top Withens' farmhouse connected
with Wuthering Heights, its cresting moor,
a red grouse, the land dreamlike fanning forth.
"Heathcliff!" In silence I cried my broken life's desire.
"I wish I were a girl again, half savage and hardy, and free –
Why am I so changed? I'm sure I should be myself were I
once among the heather on those hills."

At the Bottom of the Stairs

At the bottom of stone stairs –
garden and gold forsythia
planted by the woman who
dwelled there.

But those few who knew
knew she was a wife dying there,

and after slaps and punches
that left her face a hurricane sky
greenly darkening

she planted sprigs
of forsythia at the base
of stairs

her husband dragged her
by her long braids
down. Fast

her forsythia grew, spread
like the crazy years.
Gowned and mute
she pruned

branches trying to rise up
over Gloucester wall,
bush first to bloom
in spring.

That forsythia
men poets call gold
was never gold,

and yellow now glows
unpruned and free

as the woman's ghost
who barefoot strays
beyond the walls by Cripple Cove.

Tenderness

After four decades you appear in a dream
during this June night rain, not just any rain
but a hard downpour that shakes me

from my naked sleep, heart wracked
with an old fear, lonely and inconsolable
in this mountain night of no stars

and deer huddling in the wet dark,
invisible as I am behind my door.
"Raining cats and dogs" people call it,

hallucinations of meows and barks
piercing the mad drumming on roof, deck,
and lawn turned to meadow because

this spring it rains so much there is no
chance to mow. But I don't care, I love
the violets, buttercups, and forget-me-nots,

and the tall grass will keep safe the fawns.
After awhile the rain's rhythms rock me
back to sleep, and there ye be

with your Irish voice, melodious lilt
laced with cynicism accrued from days
of going hungry and fleeing Ireland

for New York. We greet each other inside
thatched cottage mostly bare, me smiling
in purple Irish sweater I bought from

Kathleen of Muckross, knitted in that way
my flame-haired Irish ancestresses knew,
and you wearing a sweater moss green,

its pattern to identify a man lost at sea.
Your hair glows stallion-black once more,
I swirl long torn skirt across tear-stained floor

to where you wait like a candle in a window,
kindling this wayfaring ghost with a tenderness
I had forgotten in the years I drowned.

On Your First Day of Radiation Treatment You Remember the Poet Ai

You remember when the radiation tech's female assistant
blasts you after you state your name, date of birth,
then edge into the radiation room with giant machines
color of yellowed teeth, gleaming and hanging
from the ceiling like something out of Star Trek.
You remember when you pull off blouse and camisole
to leave on chair as you had during the CAT scans
before stepping up on the little stool, wriggling
your flesh into place on the narrow table, its hole
for your left breast to hang through. You remember
when the assistant in a tone evoking Nurse Ratchet's
in *One Flew Over the Cuckoo's Nest* scolds you for not
switching into ugly cotton gown in the Changing Room,
accusing you of taking up too much precious time
by tossing your clothes aside in "the wrong room."
You remember that March Friday a friend of yours
and the poet Ai's phoned to say she had been taken
to the hospital, next day phoning again, crying
the brilliant poet had died of breast cancer.
You stunned. She had never mentioned cancer
during your correspondence about life as mixed
lineage indigenous women, Ai depressed because
her Cheyenne blood either came from a woman
Custer had lain with or one his brother, Tom,
had taken as his Indian "wife." You still hear

the friend lamenting Ai didn't like going to doctors
because of their attitude towards her, their coldness,
their tones of voice, their condescension. Sure,
you got why a woman of African, Japanese, Irish,
Cheyenne, etc., heritage felt that way. You could
feel the small scared girl trembling inside the skin
of many colors of the scarred poet who created
a brilliant diva mask for herself. Ai meaning Love.
During your first radiation treatment you remember
other women who died of breast cancer, mourn
your mother, grandmother, great grandmother,
your own mask not betraying to the braying assistant
how tomorrow you will call your oncologist
who gave you his cell phone number, praised
your poetry, told you to do whatever made you
feel comfortable, slab of meat of you making
a stand for its spirit, refusing to gown itself
with ugliness in a tyrant's changing room.

Pinktober

My mother and paternal grandmother died of breast cancer.
I am a "breast cancer survivor," such a cheery label.
Turns out my birth month, October, has been deemed
Breast Cancer Awareness Month – *Pinktober* – hear
whatever laughter lingers in me. Even pre-diagnosis
I couldn't abide the pink stuff pedaled in the name
of breast cancer awareness, the way it flashed me
back to the hell of when Mom was dying of cancer
metastasized into her liver and bones. How it made me
remember I was conceived right after Grandma died
of a tumor big as a balloon about to pop, far too young
and leaving behind ten Great Depression children.
Pink ribbon Forever stamps cause me PTSD. But
do donate to research or some hospital or organization
if you believe it can end this nightmare disease.
Better yet, be kind to a person when you learn they have
been dealt the Hanged Man card of breast cancer or any
disease, even if simply asking, "How's your soul today?"
Please be gentle. Don't tell cancer victims to eat
brown rice, stay positive (negative is best on Planet Cancer),
or otherwise preach and make it all about you,
especially on Facebook. Consider what Jesus said
about praying in public. As for me, my associations
with pink are such that I must question why women
who have endured breast cancer would wish to be
"pretty in pink" or associated with this color forced
on little girls to make them squeeze mammogram-like
into the "sugar and spice and all things nice" stereotype.

Not me. I prefer Blood Moon red, hues of the rainbow,
fall leaves painting rains and winds. Some days I revel
in being a tough old broad in New Moon black reviled
as "Bitch" or "Witch." I binge watch murder mysteries,
suspect God is nothing but a cosmic stun gun. Not to worry!
I also breathe "thank you" for everything good in my life,
including those people by my side two summers ago when
I had breast cancer surgery and three weeks of radiation
during which technicians played 1960s songs for me prone
on a high table, left tit hanging through a hole, brain recalling
virginal puppy love days before I was a slab of meat
no longer able to cry. Love to all of you who helped me
feel again to where I am unabashed about being sentimental.
Thank you for the wildflowers, garden food, books, and that kitten.
Gratitude for driving me to doctors and "what needed to be done."
Appreciation for the trip to Antarctica and regaling me with jokes
and silly stories to calve the glacier of my heart with laughter.
I would savor ice-cream with you Forever, emblazon your faces
on stamps of many colors used for love letters only.

Round Top

Usual way up is cracked road
barely wide enough for a car to carry
mourners to cemetery cascading
down mountainside whose graves
include her parents and grandparents,
everywhere in Catskills more bones
where her people go far back
and after death linger as ghosts.
Nearly seventy, she continues
to walk there, murmurs names in stone,
mingles with spirits she will soon join.
Always she is breathless once she
reaches spruces serving as fragrant
Aeolian harps for winds blowing high
above river valley and town whose gossip
the ones with dirt for mouths no longer
care about. She feels the dead's gratitude
for such music when they can miss
their bodies so and lack tongues to sing.
If only she could see again her father's
green eyes, her mother's shy Indian smile.
Beyond what Great Uncle Fred called
Boot Hill rises the Round Top proper,
the woods and princess pines,
berry bushes and caves created
by great mountain boulders toppled
over. This the trysting place
for small town lovers, where she suspects

her mother and father first made love
and conceived her eldest brother.
She keeps the sepia photograph of them
on that World War II day they came home
from that mountain, father in Marine uniform,
mother in home sewn clothes alluring enough
for a Hollywood star, posing in radiant embrace.
A smile like her mother's dazzles across
her face recalling a boy who coaxed her
down on soft moss by the caves,
unzipping her dress, blaze of hand
on naked back, his October kisses still
summer hot on the red leaf of her being
ready to fall. And roused by their desire
the cemetery's century of lovers,
surely the happiest dead in the world.

Why Did You Invite Me

(for Danielle, mother of Brodie, Danny & Ramsey)

"Why did you invite me to visit you in Florida?," you asked,
your sixteen-year-old face suffused with Bonita Springs sunlight,
skin deepening to bougainvillea-red, to the memory of Mohawk
ancestresses mocked as "redskins" by pale invaders. Far out
in the Gulf of Mexico the moon-tide crawled in long, watery lengths
to shore, crashed at our bare feet where we lounged on shell-strewn
beach. I gazed at you, Danielle – niece who called me Spirit Sister,
wrote poems and stories like me, drew and painted visions
as my mother did, dreamed in ways unique to our bloodline –
smiled at how you were always Question's child. When three,
glimpsing me naked in my bath, you asked, "Do all mommies
have fur, Aunt Susie?" How furred I felt then, a young, flushed,
female beast blurting, "Yes, they do," clutching a towel to my

bare-naked bear-ness, stepping out of the bath. Now you startled
that beast, again, blue eyes watching me like the sky-wide eyes
of that small girl in bathroom doorway leading to a future
sojourn on white beach. I smiled, "Do you know how you
wish you'd been given figure skating lessons but never were,
vowing when you have a daughter she'll learn the jumps, twirls
and wild designs denied to you? I desired the same, instead
skated on Catskill lakes, parents too poor to pay for lessons
from Olympic skaters who taught at Grossinger's Hotel.
And my mother, your grandma, never learned to skate or swim,
swore her daughters wouldn't live in fear of water and ice the way
she lived. I wanted to give to you what my mother wished to give
to me, her mother to her, and you to your yet unborn children."

"Freedom?" you asked. You rose up from beach and empty shells,
shook back your hair, auburn glints arrowing out in sun reddening
in western sky. Back and forth you waded in the water, your own
secret sea and tide. Your flesh, in scarlet bikini, disassembled
each time you glided through the sun's funneled rays, liquid
silhouette reappearing over and over again – you, but not
you – but also me, your mother, my mother, her mother, and all
the women of your line invited back by your proud, half-shy body
with its scent of pineapples. "Look, Aunt Susie!" You started
flapping your arms like the gulls and terns surrounding you.
"Look, I can fly!" You dove into a wave's clawed shimmer.
I remembered how you lamented that flying to Florida
was your first plane trip – and you sixteen! I laughed
I didn't fly until I was thirty-three, my mother never flew,
and before us our grandmothers simply stood and dreamed
after hawks and eagles high above Catskill cliffs.

Now I watched you there in the salt water, buoyed up
out of the waves like an American Aphrodite, dreaming
about your boyfriend, your "poetry man" – all week long
telling me your sunlit stories of first love. Yet only yesterday
you showed me your latest essay, charred words taking a stand
on mute pages, smoldering with sarcasm about "Lady Estrogen"
trying to stop you from staying a tomboy. "That tomboy part
is what keeps our hearts wild and makes us artists," I laughed
at how naturally you had come to flashing your eyes, tilting
your head, thrusting out one round perfect hip at passing men.

I sighed, still and glistening among empty shells.
Why did I invite you, Danielle, your strong dreamer's body
in the Gulf of Mexico reflecting the descending sun like fire?
Because the furred beast ages. Because, little Spirit Sister,
daughter of Poetry, there will never be another visitation like this.

PART II

"Thanks to life"

Gracias a la Vida (Violeta Parra)

Dreamscape, Nova Scotia

Once in Nova Scotia, the dreams changed
along with landscape and soundscape.

Land touched sea more, and the salty
Atlantic touched back with coves and bays.

There was something of lovemaking in the air
and people talked to strangers like herself –

smiling, polite, kind. She laughed to them,
"You are all so courteous," not meaning it

in a cynical New York way. "You're nice
like the people I grew up with in the Catskills,"

she'd marvel, and they were not offended
by being called "nice" the way some of her

sophisticated and cynical friends would be.
In this country no one was quick to take offense

or give it. Camping, nights she dreamed about
the children like the little girl who held open

the door for her at Walmart – and the small
Mi'kmac boy whose mother brought him into

the last campsite's ladies room, his shy grin
when he glanced back at her before skipping out

the door into a sunny morning. She dreamed
about the innocent faces she thought had been

lost to children forever. Loons trilled their low
blues on the lakes and rivers. One dawn

she watched an eagle swoop down then fly up
clutching an eel in its talons – later glimpsed

a bull moose foraging close to cliff-side trail,
its head and mountainous rack bowed to earth.

Before leaving Nova Scotia, she dreamed
she held a miniature eagle in her cupped hands,

having a conversation without words.
The bird shape-shifted into a rainbow trout,

spots glowing like Van Gogh brush strokes.
Soon she was painting the sky, moon,

and falling stars in hues from another universe.
Waking from sleep she still felt Eagle and Trout

in her palms, the one who soars high
and the one who dives deep.

L'Anse aux Meadows, Newfoundland

Once woodland, green sweet grasses now –
last September flowers like tiny suns,
yellow constellations dotting breeze blown
peninsula where Leif Eriksson and other Vikings
lingered for three years, maybe ten, before they
realized its merciless winters and fierce Skraelings
were too much even for them. Norse women

and Norsemen sailed to North American continent
in the year 1000, nearly five centuries before Columbus.
The vast meadow undulates in mounds from where
huts and workshops once perched on stone foundations,
beyond land's edge the Labrador Sea – and to the East
Atlantic Ocean, where iridescent blues of water
and sky glow unlike any blues I have beheld before.

Stunned by my lack of language for this color,
strangely I want to weep, wondering if those Vikings
saw the same hues and felt as overwhelmed by such beauty
as they did by indigenous warriors catapulting mysterious
spheres at them from a heaven-blue pole. Only Freydis,
eight months pregnant, Eric the Red's flame-haired daughter,
dared to confront the Skraelings, whipping her left breast

out of her bodice, slapping it with her sword, terrifying
the Natives with her ice floe of a tit until they fled
to their boats, paddling fast away from her battle cry.

So Eirik's Vinland Saga tells it. I tell you this,
L'Anse aux Meadows *is* magical, any violent clashes
between Vikings and Skraelings swallowed up
by centuries of forgetting. I tell you

there I beheld my first iceberg like an azure beacon
in the Labrador Sea, a point of lonely stillness asking
"What's the point of it all?" I am far too old to answer
such a plaintive question. Long ago I dreamed of that
peninsula metamorphosed to mounded meadows
from whence poems are born a far north blue, where
I suspect Vikings and Indians made brave love at last.

Queen Anne's Lace, Cape Breton

Queen Anne's lace flames by on Cape Breton's roads,
thicker than she imagined that flower her mother loved
could grow – each a dainty dance in breeze easing
in from sea, bright in sun but somehow brighter
in Nova Scotia rains. Riding past, she re-sees
doilies her mother used to crochet, intricate
circles shaped like what her Ma dubbed
the Lady Flower. She placed them all about
the house, under lamps and bowls and vases.
The rest she gave away. Every room seemed
a bride with pure dreams.

Queen Anne's lace curtsies in Cape Breton's
air fragrant with spruce and sweetness distilled
from all its evergreens, blossoms, berries.
Most people no longer breathed such air,
she shuddering when she can't quite forget
the cities back in America, hate spreading
as much as breast cancer once metastasized
into her mother's bones. Her mother saw it
coming, forewarned how they would lose
their freedoms more and more. Yet
she kept on smiling at what others scorned –

"the little things in life" – rapturous when
Queen Anne's lace bloomed among wild chicory
adding lavender-blues to white. Oh, Mom,
I wish you were here with me to see

the flower like you, a lady – many ladies
in a world grown too cruel and rude.
Along the heaved roads, too, signs in both
English and Gaelic, evoking Scotland and Ireland,
ancient homes. And the people in kinship
with her mother's flower, glowing in sun
and somehow in rain even brighter.

Three Pub Crawl, Sydney, Cape Breton

Driving in, her lover spotted an eagle in rain,
stopped so she could photograph its splendor
on a bare branch, bird and old tree
mist-softened to silver. Back
in the Catskills, her people say seeing
the great bald eagle brings good luck,
and she carried that spell to Sydney visit
with Hassan, a friend's friend, and Bruce,
his Nova Scotia boyfriend.

What a world, hey? Her roving companion
and she come all the way from New York State,
wandering up to Prince Edward Island then
Nova Scotia, all the way out to Cape Breton –
she a mountain Indian, her lover from Brooklyn,
Bruce a Glace Bay native with Irish roots,
and Hassan a Syrian who met Jim, our friend,
in Montreal. Jim said Hassan was a beautiful man
we might wish to meet.

Despite sorrows she still has a mad crush
on this crazy world in which she can hop in
a car or plane then find herself with people
as new and startling and lovely to her
as an eagle gazing across a strait
in rain. Yet in another way she is
forever homesick because her fate

is to roam and leave what passes
for home again and again, trusting
gentle humans may offer safe sojourns.

So it was with meeting Hassan and Bruce
taking them to three pubs for food and drink
and music worthy of a wild sea place,
for her fish 'n chips and her first poutine.
And damned if the Guinness-on-tap didn't taste
the same as Guinness she drank in Ireland
three rapturous springs ago. The Governor's,
Daniel's, and Old Triangle Irish Alehouse –
the Pourhouse, the Snug, Tigh Tan Cheoil,
as in Ireland all signs including Gaelic.

The bands and singing too loud,
but the voices of two new friends
play in her heart like strands of ancient songs
from lands left behind but not forgotten
anymore than she can forget Hassan speaking
of Aleppo, his mother and other family members
trapped in Syria, nightmare of the ones still there –
and Bruce telling her outside Hassan's hearing
how he felt when he first saw his boyfriend's eyes

burning above a fire he had made behind
his house for a party, how he hoped this affair
would not die to ash after he had been so hurt
by other men. O Hassan was beautiful
as Jim said – Bruce equally so.
What a great country, hey, where likely
no one would jail or murder them –

Bruce in jaunty straw hat
and Hassan chain-smoking
("Worst doctor ever," Bruce jokes)
while smoldering beneath neon lights?

Eagle in Cape Breton rain.
Good fortune on a fogbound night.

Morning in Cape Breton

Morning in Cape Breton, we hike
three miles out to cliffs and sea
through a trio of climate zones –
temperate, boreal, taiga –

where evergreens don't grow high,
close to ocean and salty winds
blasting in. Black spruces lace
air with fragrance like long ago
Christmas trees, sweet as first love,

until birches break them apart –
there a bull moose grazes,
black ravens chat on a white branch,
miniature raspberry patches redden
path edge. I pluck a few raspberries
to give to you, a few for myself.

Eventually, we glimpse sea.
In increasing wind we stagger
down boardwalk steps, you
disappearing in rain and mist.
Blueberries huddle low and little
against the ground.

I pluck one Taiga blueberry,
body of the Great Mystery to place
in my mouth that wants to sing
then howl. I fear you loped off

to one of those forbidden places
you can't resist, worry the wind
might knock you into fierce waves
to dream with drowned fishermen.

But there you rise, a wraith in fog,
while I who have lost so many so fast
blink back tears from my rain-wet face.
Gaily I tell you about the blueberries,

you tease it's forbidden to eat them
in a National Park. No regrets, I say.
That Taiga blueberry was the best berry
I've ever had. You kneel to taste one, too,
our tongues sky blue.

Shawanditha

Traveling through Newfoundland, it seems as if
you slipped out of America and light years away
into a dimension magical, as though you had died
and winged to this strange north where the garbage
of your country's politicians, the loud crass lies
of the rich intending to make citizens slaves,
ebb out like flotsam and jetsam on Dawnland
sea, during sunny days the waves like dreams
drowning dark memories, and the sky, the sky –
never have you met such blue, your vocabulary
of azure, sapphire, turquoise, tourmaline, indigo
unable to fit that hue metamorphosing you
to mute sparkles. And maybe because

in this maritime world you shine unbound,
you keep meeting nice people, yes, *nice*,
until your man starts teasing them,
"Is there a law on this big rock that says
people have to be sweet?" No one here
is quick to take offense, no one hints
of carrying a handgun, no one swears –
you swear the inhabitants of this berry land
are fools like you, forever quick to smile.
And the Indigenous don't appear
to wage inter-tribal warfare the way
colonized Indians try to vanish other Indians
in the Disunited States of divide-and-conquer.

Speaking of vanishing, bit by bit
you learn about the Native Beothuk
who centuries ago roamed over this island,
skins reddened by ocher into perpetual sunrises
in a timeless time of such abundance
that one could scoop up a net full of cod
close to shore, dig mussels for breakfast,
and during winters have plenty of caribou meat
to eat. Quiet markers point out old graves
or camping grounds. Museum signs and scenes
behind glass reflect your shocked face
across the words telling the trail of how
they went extinct. The last Beothuk
a young woman – Shawanditha.
Died of TB in St. John's, 1829.

"Shawanditha, Shawanditha," you whisper
inside your heart her name whenever
fiord winds whip up a nest of wildness
in your long hair, tangles you can't
comb out. "Shawanditha," when you stoop
to pick blueberries and cloudberries,
or reach higher for gooseberries dangling
like shiny ornaments off lush bushes,
a thanksgiving of late summer sweetness
lavishing your tongue. "Shawanditha"
when you spot a bull moose, see puffins
with day-glo orange beaks catch capelins,
brake for red fox kits playing on a night road,
unafraid while you and your companion watch.

You imagine how the last Beothuk "full blood"
would have loved to roam around Newfoundland
in this way you are rambling with your man,
sleeping sometimes in a tent and crawling out
under opal stars where the Milky Way still spills
across a lucid night sky and the Great Bear
nearly touches Mother Earth and you feel
the Mystery that birthed storytelling
around the campfires of the first beginning.
Yes, this enchanted land where the extinct
once believed that after death they canoed
to the Place of the Good Spirit and would
forever fish and hunt, feast and sing –

where you are Shawanditha in the Spirit Place.

Aurora Borealis, Goose Bay, Labrador

(for the Brown family)

You were hoping to be graced
by the Northern Lights once you took
the night ferry to Labrador, although
it was September so you weren't sure
the ancient sky dancers would come
when winter had not yet blown in. You
could only imagine how winter must be
in that province of black spruces, low lying
berry bushes, and white moose lichen
lightening the rocks. And those gravel roads
should anyone be crazy enough to go there,
during rains sharp stones splashing up
from car and truck wheels, cracking hard
against windows, leaving mud enough
that between that and rain and mist
all road disappears and it is as if ghosts
have taken over and you are one of them.
Not ten miles in before you felt a loneliness
stranger than you had ever felt before.

No caribou to be seen. A few birds.
You camped out by ocean the first night
when that day's rain stopped, and in
the clearing mist you saw what natives call
a fogbow, an arc of many colors soaring

from sea to sky and back down to beach.
And not just a single fogbow, a double
then several others, and you chanting
"Wow, Wow, Wow" in the chilling dusk.
Fuckin' freezing that night in the tent, you
wanting to kick your snoring companion
who thought it "a great idea to camp out
in this beautiful ocean-side spot."
Maybe it was three when you had to pee,
shivering groped your way outside
onto the sand and squatting peered up.
And not since Guatemala decades ago
had you beheld that many stars so big,
so bright, it seemed you could raise
your hand and pick a bouquet of light.
You re-entered the tent in love again.
You and your roving companion agreed
you probably would not be able to keep

camping out in such raw, wet weather.
After some days you made it to Goose Bay
and thanks to Couchsurfing stayed with
a Métis daughter, mother and father.
Back home in Catskills such people
are called "part Indian," like you.
As with other Métis you had met
in Canadian Maritime, Robin, Sheila,
and Harold were open, smiling and kind,
same as long ago mountain Indians
you grew up around. The first night you
and your companion cooked tacos for them.
Second night they did the cooking,

a feast of bear meat and salted beef,
juneberry biscuits, potatoes, carrots, corn,
a lavish supper like their Sunday jigs.
And stories for dessert, including

Harold describing how earlier that week
he drove back to his cabin in the woods
where he was regaled by the most beautiful
Aurora Borealis he had ever beheld,
so many vivid hues. And when he
talked-sang about the dazzling sky
you felt yourself there, streamers of red, blue,
green, violet, yellow shimmering over you
and across the wild land of your heart.
That Labrador night transported you back
to 1950s' Catskills, to the men who hunted
and fished and understood everything about
woods and water, animals and birds, to women
who gathered leeks, berries, nuts, and apples
and still knew medicine, and to young Natives
like yourself who couldn't wait to leave
for neon-lit cities and faraway countries
where a dreamer could wander forever,
as if love and being Indian weren't enough.

Oda a los Copos de Nieve
(Ode to the Snowflake)

Santiago, Chile, streets –
jacaranda trees freeing their petals
in December light which must be
the light people sing about
after near death experiences
when they fly through their skins
in an astonishment of wings lifting
them above snow-capped Andes,
gaze with condor eyes down
on their breathless bodies and everybody,
love soaring enough to pick hatred
clean. Streets where Pablo Neruda
swayed like a big-bellied boat, in Bellavista
clambering hill house he dream-built
for Mathilde of the red hair which refused
to behave. In this city of seven million
flaming towards summer solstice
I wander with my own lover
whose hair refuses servitude
to the taming comb. Hugging
sidewalk shadows whenever we can,
we embrace each other in places
purpled by fallen jacaranda flowers,
overhead green parrots squawking
the poetry of lost trees. And what if
I died in the Catskill Mountains last May
when I was diagnosed with breast cancer?

Could Santiago, Chile, be my after life?
Is this light the Milky Way's star road
watched over by llama eyes, this flashing
out of my skin not my usual fleeting rapture
when solstice flares in? Back home
on Facebook Timelines friends share
photographs of America's first snows.
But others post right-wing meme lynchings
hoping to strangle the gentle with taunts –
"You're too sensitive. Bunch of snowflakes.
Stop whining." Sí, maybe I died up north,
but surely not from the tortures of crass words
administered by the pseudo-clever.
On this iridescent day Santiago is my heaven
in which Chilean poet-ghosts amble with my lover
and me. I sing the names of Gabriela Mistral,
Nicanor and Violeta Parra, Pablo Neruda
and Mathilde whose wild hair made him
wilder, and many others. I praise all
the sensitive ones, including the Indians
in this land shaped like a dagger.
Undefeated we smile at snow
like fire opal necklaces encircling
mountain peaks, liberating our eyes
from the old existence in which politics
seemed important, freeing us from
the mean-spirited who politicize
even snowflakes, whose only religion
is to condemn anyone who defies
the god of fast food clichés. I laugh
"¡*Salud*!" to the rebels of extravagant heart
who sparkle unique as each snowflake.

I sing those crystals that gather
into shape-shifting clouds until
they descend in countless soft silences
of the people who have never been heard,
a wordless music of snow covering
the hard land. In this Chilean heat
I praise the snowflakes that seem
so delicate, so transient, but possess
the power of nor'easters and when
they melt become powerful rivers
flowing into the seas, water growing
forests and crops. In this city of sun
and shadow and forgotten secrets
I remember when my lover and I
fell to Mother Earth and snowflakes
like tiny birds shivered on our lips,
how our arms turned to wings and we
made snow angels in a new world.

At the Museo Violeta Parra in Santiago, Chile, I Remember

December 2017, summer blooming in Santiago, Chile –
but at the Museo Violeta Parra I thought of winter 1978
in upstate Binghamton, New York, me a 28 year old poet
who had dropped in and out of college during a decade
of bedazzling ideals. Marching against Vietnam War
on D.C. streets, holding peace vigils with Quakers outside
White House fence, balling lovers with hair long as mine
and traveling cross-country in *de rigueur* VW van seemed
an apt education for a Catskill Indian girl of many "bloods"
like ley lines singing to others of entranced heart everywhere.

But by January 1978 I had returned to college, a Literature
and Creative Writing major at the State University Center
at Binghamton, New York, nearly infamous for its brilliant
students from middle class and poor families, struggling
outsiders who were visionary, compassionate, radical –
myself so fucking poor I only ate once a day, quelling
hunger with coffee, waiting in subzero temperatures for
blue buses to sweep me away to brick building classrooms
then back to Susquehanna River Valley where I rented
a tiny Endicott efficiency, to reading far past midnight,

including Nicanor Parra books my Creative Writing professor
told me about, *Emergency Poems* and *Poems and Antipoems*.
Nicanor became my friend that winter I was alone, sunk
in my tattered chair or curling up on sagging narrow bed
that came with the place, off and on through nor'easter nights

catching myself when I started to fall off mattress edge
and out of my dreams onto bare floor. But Parra, that winter's
soulmate, understood how poverty and hunger get fed up
with the smirking words of the rich, want to strip naked
the similes, metaphors, and confining rhymes of professors

babbling "equality for all" at faculty cocktail parties
while deaf to the desperation that begs for a poetry of howl
in the tongues of people so unequal they forget how to speak.
My writing professor never mentioned Nicanor's sister, Violeta,
and I wondered about his neglect in the Santiago museum
dedicated to her vivid art, lyrics and music. Before making
my pilgrimage often I listened to Violeta sing her sublime
"Gracias a la Vida," "Thanks to Life," felt her to be my friend
as Nicanor was in the subarctic, lonely winter of 1978.
Young woman then – old woman in Museo dedicated

to the activist who defied all oppression by thanking life
as we do in our Iroquois ceremony of inviting in all the spirits
of Earth, Water, Air, Sky, thanking them for their gifts.
Upon leaving, I rested under a jacaranda tree, purple petals
dropping on me the way snow fell one morning in 1978
when I waited an eternity for the blue bus, could not cease
shivering until I wept, tears ice jewels on my frozen cheeks –
giving up on going to class, trudging in thickening blizzard
back to my room and a half to curl up with old quilt
and *Emergency Poems*, face blazing into radiant defiance.

Gracias a los dos poetas, Violeta *y* Nicanor.

68th October Birthday, Santiago, Chile

We are staying with new friends in Santiago, Chile –
Alberto, Isabel, and daughter, Almendra, well named
because her teenage eyes actually appear like almonds,
the largest and brownest in world history. Alberto
from Spain – poets like me can see he stepped
out of a Renaissance painting in the Prado, weary
of being a prince striking a dignified pose inside
a gilded frame for an eternity of pretentious art critics
and neglected matrons wishing their husbands were
that elegant. The dawn he escaped led him to Isabel
with her black hair which like the family cat never turns
completely tame, long strands breaking loose in such
rapturous curls that Alberto followed them all the way
to Santiago where Isabel greeted him with lips so plush
every word she spoke blossomed like a kiss. And this

brings us to the eve of my 68th birthday on Earth
in what I call the Mirror America, to an October
which in Santiago is spring – *primavera* in her prime,
when the jacaranda and calla lilies bloom
and parrots flash neon green through the trees.
And on this birthday cusp our new friends
invite their old friends and family members
to dinner, people of various generations, lineages,
and lands, including Isabel's Mapuche poet Papa –
and of course he and I serve everyone appetizers
of Mohawk and Mapuche metaphors, images and rhyme.

Isabel's 85 year old *abuela* loves my *blanco* hair,
thinks I am her classmate, and we walk hand in hand
like two little schoolgirls long ago.

Sí, we are conversing, hugging, laughing –
spontaneously dancing to music Alberto plays
in this high apartment in a neighborhood
of murals, multi-colored playgrounds, and children
who still skip outside to swing and fly down slides.
Sweetly wild we smile in rooms rich with books, CDs
and old LPs, while the ghosts of revolutionary poets weep
beneath the balcony wishing they could shout "¡*Salud*!"
once more. Our governments demand we hate each other,
but instead we are forgetfully feral and loving. At midnight
everyone sings "Happy Birthday" in English, then *Español*,
each time laughing "Make three wishes" before twice
I blow out candle flames in a flamboyance of six wishes.

Valparaíso, City of Murals, Poetry, Dream Streets, Love at First and Last Sight

Not the city church-going Christians dream about.
Not the celestial city of pearly gates, gold streets
on infinite flat grids, walls of jasper whose green
is insomniac eyes jealous of rebels daring to fly
Lucifer-like away from the God of erratic rage
and bearded sadism eager to condemn people
to hell fires and tortures forever. Not the city
of the God of no vacations, but Valparaiso

the Vivid, city of murals, poetry, dream streets,
of love at first sight and last sight where anyone
can migrate to walk her mountainside streets veering
like the imaginations of artists, poets, musicians,
songlines in the Chilean light shining up and down
and at crazy angles penetrating sacred circles
of primary Pachamama colors. Valparaiso, city
of visions painted by extravagant hands

across walls, gates, on sidewalks, alleys, steep
stairs, inside courtyards and hidden hearts
and secret voices. City where men and women
remember they were born with wings whenever
they ascend steps emblazoned with sunflowers,
parrots, piano keys, where children smile at walls
and gates dissolved by penguins, whales, guanacos,
Mapuche Indians dancing an ancient freedom.

Not the city of sedentary angels plucking harps
but a crazy quilt of enthralling imperfections where
any day or night another earthquake could shake
the mountain and churn the bay waters into tidal waves,
city of feral dogs who howl from dusk to dawn
recalling they were once wolves, their shit everywhere
on the disobedient streets, Valparaiso of lovers
fucking by cracked windows overlooking urban lights

descending like shooting stars to the port of sailors
and prostitutes, orgasms like earthquakes every time. Not
the padlocked afterlife where pseudo saint, Peter, would stone
a *poetisa* like me and kick the companion I call Raised by Wolves,
but Valparaiso the Voluptuous embracing us because I dress
like a mural and my mate is a wild ecstatic wanderer,
valiant city *de puta madre* drunk on pisco sours, Neruda's,
Mistral's, the Parras' poetry on sky blue plaques defying walls.

Eating Ice-Cream in Valparaiso, Chile, with Federico García Lorca

(for Oscar Houck)
("If death is death, what then of poets, and of sleeping things,
    if no one remembers them?" Lorca)

How like a poet to show up when ice-cream is involved,
even a dead one like you, Federico. Of course this *poetisa*
remembers you, as do countless others who love your words
possessing the wings of condors. Thank you for flying
from Andalusia when you saw me dreaming by a doorway
in Valparaiso, outside an *heladería* called *Poesía de Sabor*,
Poetry of Flavor, in an extravaganza of mirror announcements,
a tango of two elegant scripts on swirlings of multi-hued wall
encircling bright tile with your blue verse musing about
la rosa y la aurora. Dearest Lorca, it feels like dawn when
you blaze down on this serpentine street of stucco walls
displaying fragments of your poems on the gay colors of *casas*
in sun and shadow just as in your native Granada. Brother
ice-cream lover, this morning my heart is the tile's azure rose.

I'll treat, Federico. What kind of ice-cream cone do you desire?
What would you, famous ghost, genius spirit, relish? Ah, a dip
of double-chocolate! Perhaps you hear dark sounds in chocolate,
taste *duende* when it is doubled, more intense. I, myself, choose
a gelato dubbed *Oda a un Limon* after Neruda's poem, Pablo who
once lived several blocks distant in La Sebastiana and with whom
you shared a friendship of holy fire. I welcome "a universe of gold,"
"a goblet of miracles," for I have journeyed five thousand miles from

los Estados Unidos now divided in an angry god's nightmare of collapsing
stars, in a collective nervous breakdown where poets are not needed
except as scapegoats. How delicious to share this shade with you,
to cool our irrepressible tongues and smile cat-like at Chilean men
with hair blacker than yours, Lorca, on this mountain of murals
where we have never been hurt and it is the first innocent hour on Earth.

Abrazos for Two Mapuche Men

Abrazos for the man whose house we came upon
after a day of wandering among Chilean volcanoes,
when we needed shelter and he happened to be
renting out rooms in the midst of forested land
still mostly indigenous. I give my embrace
two years later, recalling how tired I was
the night I stumbled after John into a home
that felt of vastness, the gentleman leading us
to our upstairs bedroom with a balcony
then back down to brightly lit kitchen
where John later cooked spaghetti and offered
some to our host. But not until morning
when I was rested did my eyes wend their way
to framed photographs of the man and others
in Native regalia, and then to a woman's dress,
headdress and beads draped behind glass –
"*Mi madre*," he gestured. I admired the pictures
of his family and friends, asked if he would mind
posing with me by the dress his mother once danced in.
"*Sí!*" – while John translated for us, the man speaking
about the Mapuche and I about the Mohawk people,
marveling over our similar cultures and histories.
At first shy in how we posed, so dignified, so proud,
we soon ventured peace symbols, and by the time
we came to the last picture we raised our arms
with "power to the people" fists. He told us

corporations wanted to steal more Mapuche land
and cut down their trees. I asked him about
the longhouse-like building with turquoise roof
that I gazed down upon after waking that morning –
painted with the sun, the moon and the stars.
As I thought, it was a Mapuche ceremonial house.
He explained the cosmology expressed by symbols
within circles, while I spoke of the Iroquois creation story
and Turtle Island. *Abrazos para ti, mi querido hermano,*
for I shall never forget how you hugged me, my brother,
in a way that sang everything deep down beneath
your Spanish words and my English language.
Even writing this two years later I smile, yet also
could cry and cry and cry.

II.

Abrazos for Moises who showed up at the Lighthouse of Murals
in Huasco, Chile, after John and I wandered down to the Pacific,
intrigued by the surreal sight of a lighthouse painted in
variations of blue, mostly – images of the village spilling
down to ocean mating with sky and all the sea creatures
beneath the waves and mermaid apparitions as well as a great
haunting face of an indigenous person whose age and gender
were elusive, hands lifted upwards, arrowheads flying past
coppery naked body. I suppose the question is – how
do we find each other, we who have this way of dreaming
and feeling and loving and embracing, possess this elusive
quality that most people would see as disappearing mists
whereas it is powerful and forever radiant. How is it we
simply start chatting and soon we are sharing stories,
sculptures, paintings, music and poetry? Yes, as soon

as I learned this beautiful man of the black tumbling hair
and eyes brown as the most secret, deep, and sacred places
of Mother Earth, Pachamama, I walked back to our car
to get a book of my poetry for him, the one about freedom,
the one called *Car Stealer* with the horses of holy fire
galloping across its front cover. Moises the Mapuche,
another indigenous brother, man who picked up his flute
and played notes I miss every day of my existence, sounds
of the spirit that modern life tells us doesn't exist, melodies
of the universes of every cell in our bodies – message
we shall never be defeated no matter who tries to shatter
our hearts. Moises who reminded me how lonely it feels
when no one really looks anymore at another human being
as he gazed at me, into me – that despite all, a love survives
that can shake us to the very roots until we blaze up through
genocide into being as the sun, the moon, and the stars.
Moises whose wife was dying of cancer and yet managed
to smile and be kind to us, to me who had breast cancer
not long ago. Moises who gifted me one of his sculptures
that cradled sun rays and moonshine in desert rock.
Moises who gave us a music CD and miniature lighthouse
so we could take the Lighthouse of Murals of the Village
of Huasco home with us. Moises whose wife died after I
returned home. Moises the Mapuche whose hug of hidden
tears when we said *"Adiós"* was nearly unbearable,
daring my heart to feel intensely and bravely again.
Abrazos para ti, mi querido hermano. And this poem.

That Day at Alpaca Tegualda, Chile (for Ignacio and Bonni)

That day at Alpaca Tegualda, Chile, I fell in love with alpacas
still exotic to me come all the way from New York State
en los Estados Unidos – along country road finding
a lone, lovingly polished, wooden sign pointing up to
what might be a place where John and I could buy more
Mapuche weavings made of Alpaca fur, gifts for the people
back home. An Indian woman many roads ago had told us
its name, although even after stopping in town to get more
directions from government officials, we were once more
in the throes of "Now where the fuck are we?"

And then ALPACA TEGUALDA in tall bright letters
like white alpacas. We followed ascending dirt driveway
to what we sought, multi-colored alpacas grazing behind split
wood fence, gazing curiously at us alien creatures when we
stumbled out of our dusty car, returning their stares with awe.
A sweet-faced woman appeared, next a gentleman –
Bonni and Ignacio who owned the farm – not Mapuche
but an American and Chilean who met abroad during
the Pinochet years of *los desaparecidos*, the disappeared.
Soon Our Lady of the Alpacas was reciting their love story

which began in Algeria, how passion ignited two strangers
from countries thousands of miles apart. She turned to
her husband listening from behind black-rimmed glasses
shadowing his face tanned and creased into a story skin
by South American sun. "You tell them," she urged softly.

"Tell them what they did to you when you were a young student with dreams of a good life for everyone." While mother alpacas nursed babies, he described being arrested by Pinochet's thugs, blindfolded, driven in a hurtling dark until everything stopped, rough hands dragging and dumping him in a basement of other dreamers selected for the death of all dreaming.

"I saw them beat people, heard screams, watched them drag comrades back up the stairs to be shot where no civilized eyes could bear witness. This made me wonder if we might cease being civilized if we did survive." His tears reflected sunshine, eyes sparkling as they must have shone when he was a kind boy. "Of course, you see me here, see me as one of the lucky ones. My father, a lawyer, had connections, got me released and onto a plane flying across the Atlantic. But my friends could not fly. *Lucky*," he echoed in a voice quavering with lost music. "I can never cease feeling guilty over my comrades who disappeared." We two women and two men ambled closer to fence and alpacas, some newly shorn. I edged fingers through fence opening, a baby of spiky brown fur nuzzling them, believing I could feed it milk. "You may walk among them, alpacas won't hurt you," smiled Bonni the weaver of intricate Alpaca scarves, sweaters and hats. We entered, bringing hands in enthrallment to camelid beauty, stroking sun-dappled bodies. Ignacio drifted away to the house, we drifted among newborn life. "Alpacas are not like sheep when shorn. Shearing must be done differently because they are high spirited, can't be totally tamed." That day at Alpaca Tegualda — surprised by survivors inhabited by the spirits of the beautiful alpacas.

Wild Donkeys of Chile's Atacama Desert

Wild donkeys of Chile's Atacoma Desert, I dreamed you
before I knew you existed. Since my Indian grandpa
took me one midsummer's night to watch donkey baseball
on 1950s small town ball field, this electric-lit dream
of donkeys inhabited the girl I was, poor girl enraptured
by a whirl of donkey bodies kicking up mirages of fairy dust.

Shy donkeys grazing not far from shimmering Pacific,
ever since that amazed child wished you had no riders
but could wander free as I roamed in forests and fields,
I dreamed that someday I would meet the donkeys
of no saddles or reins. Yes, a donkey would appear
as a pony did one August midnight outside our back door,

sidle over to me beneath the falling stars
until my face would fall softly against its soft face,
twinned eyes glowing as though we had just been born.
Ungrammatical donkeys of Atacama, in eighth grade
my English teacher gave me Jimenez's *Platero and I.*
After reading it, more than before I yearned to rove

with my own donkey soul mate for making memoir,
companion stubborn and sensitive as the poet
I had already become. Sí, a wind-tousled amigo
who I would not burden with packs of *nada*, nor whip
or tie down. Brown-eyed donkeys of Pachamama's desert,
your eyes evoke the dark pools in my Catskill woods,

hidden places only dreamers like me can find.
How magical the donkeys of Atacoma! If only I had
wildflowers to feed you and braid into crowns encircling
your long listening ears. Oh, silver donkey, turning
your face to me while you get a sly hard on, let us go now
to the blue sea of black rocks Neruda loved.

Mother and Daughter, Gabriela Mistral Library, La Serena, Chile

How could it have been otherwise than for John and me
to wander into the Gabriela Mistral Library after we visited
the museum dedicated to her, that library of countless windows
and a plenitude of light, that complement of books and high
balcony above where the great *poetisa* once dreamed and wrote?

How could it be otherwise than to wander into a room
where a slide show was ending, glimpse of guanacos
before the screen went dark. And John, who unlike me
knows Spanish, asked a woman of long hair and brave face
radiant in a way too many women have lost,

"¿De *qué se trata esto? ¿Por qué hay fotografías de guanacos
en toda la biblioteca?*" Wondering about the gathering
and blown up photographs of Chile's soft brown guanacos
among the bookshelves and outside gleaming in the fierce sun.
Then she told us about the pueblo of her birth, place

she grew up in, homeland of a tiny blue flower shy
among rocks, cactus blooms greeting spring with red
the color of the people's collective heart, wild donkeys,
foxes, desert and mountains stretching to Pacific Ocean
a surprise at the edge of desolation, azure and aquamarine

sparked to white fire by springtime sun. She beckoned
her daughter also of long hair and brave face, and with
the sea's salt tears in their defiant melodious voices
they told us about the corporation that bought a vastness
of earth there so they could mine it. Always the big corporation.

Always the heartless and the faceless who did such things
against the people's wishes. The mine that would rape
Pachamama, cause the guanacos to die and rare flowers
to disappear forever, its poisons that would seep into the sea
and massacre the whales and dolphins. We embraced

each other, raised right fists high while our left hands
made peace symbols. That day in the country of the people
who love their poets, in the Library of Gabriela Mistral,
in a room of rhymes and new friends from two Americas,
in that moment of solidarity how I missed my mother.

Petrified Forest, Patagonia

Unlike Argentina's pampas, the Patagonian Steppe
reveals native animals not killed to extinction
so the *estancias* of the rich can feed soft-eyed cows
who will then feed the red meat lovers of this country
of the disappeared. We even passed a sign pointing
in hand painted words to a reserve for Native people,
so isolated in its dirt vastness it seemed like a moon
crashed to Earth. How we rejoiced at that sign
and at guanacos with rheas by their tawny sides,
forever running away from human approach.

A great distance south we spotted a second sign,
Bosques Petrificados National Park, 24 kilometers
beyond road already 200 miles from any pueblo.
Of course we swerved into it, our mission to answer
every call of the wild, bouncing over gravel under sky's
far-end-of-the-world *azul* and sinking sun a light show
of cloud-shattered rays. My left breast ached where
the cancer was found nine months ago, *just scar tissue*
rubbed by my seat belt I told myself, relieved

when we stopped and an emerald-eyed ranger let us
wander through the Petrified Forest even though
it was closing time. Hiking up high strange hill
of araucaria trees felled by fierce volcanic winds
and buried by ash at Jurassic Age end, the country
of my body was also petrified forest, mute as those
60 million year old monkey puzzle trees. And might my
stunned atoms turn to quartz-like crimsons and golds,
cancer memories metamorphose into a magnificent forgetting?

I photographed my roving companion, he me.
Maybe if I posted the pictures on Facebook next time
we got Internet, the people I used to call friends and family
would click on *Likes* and *Hearts*, remind me I was real
and hadn't died but was still smiling in that life
I once believed in. Against the ranger's advice
we drove on to what he warned was remotest Patagonia,
desolation broken by ragged brush, a black butte,
night of huddling in our cradle of mud-spattered Subaru
rocked by icy winds and fall sleet, abandoning ourselves
to a starless sleep lit by nothing but a crazy love.

Traveling to the End of the World

(for Jorge Rabassa)

After leaving Petrified Forest on gravel road
the ranger and two amigos warned us
penetrated Patagonia's most isolated region,
John and I laughed at the scientists joking,
"We'll pray for you," when we decided to take
the back way out. Jorge the geologist grinned,
"Let's all have a beer in Ushuaia *if you make it*.
I live and work there and will be back tomorrow."
"*When* we make it, many beers!" I bragged bravely
before my love and I drove beyond the west side
of the kaleidoscope of marbled stumps and logs,
monkey puzzle trees metamorphosed to enchantments
of color by the alchemy of centuries. Setting sun
already kissed the jagged buttes, last rays torching
lower horizon stretching over a hundred kilometers
before Ruta 3 would arrow further south to
Tierra del Fuego. Just past National Park border
we settled on a hilly rise for our sacred place
to have a picnic then sleep in dusty Subaru –
icy rain, clouds, gale winds increasing with dusk,
just enough light for eating cheese, nuts and apples
before burrowing inside sleeping bags. Made sure
I grabbed a bottle of Malbec for extra warming,
so of course I woke in the deep of the night
and needed to pee. Squatting on puddling road
I peered up to where the clouds spread, also –

hopeful clearing where Southern constellation
twinkled down at me wondering again why I was
doing this *loco* trip, stars like mammogram image
of calcifications in my left breast the doctors diagnosed
as cancer the previous May. My thought then?
"How exquisite those calcifications look, delicate
and opalescent as snow crystals or distant stars."
Not until late that night did I weep –
remembering my mother dying of breast cancer
invading her bones, her whisper one day when chemo
dripped into her veins, "I wished I had lived a different life.
I haven't done what I dreamed. I have never even flown
in a plane." I sobbed over her and women countless
as stars whose only "end of the world" was to die not
turning feral, not casting off aprons, bras, taming lies
and the slow drips of poisonous fear. Sí, I could write
a book titled *Epiphanies While Peeing in the Middles
of Nowheres in the Midsts of Wild Nights*.
Drenched by Patagonian drizzle, muddied, wind-blasted
back into car, body shivering into a sad second sleep –
but six nights later clinking *vasos de cerveza*
in an Ushuaia restaurant overlooking Beagle Channel
where Darwin once "made it," John, Jorge and I
swapping freedom tales in Tierra del Fuego,
me toasting "¡*Salud*!" to my mother who had gone
even farther.

Antarctica Blues

Sailing on a Russian ship leaving Beagle Channel,
she clung to deck rail with other tourists who chose
that boat because it carried scientists who would
lecture about Antarctica twice a day and accompany
the less knowledgeable whenever it proved possible
to leave awhile for meeting seals and whales
sleek in the ice-studded sea or saunter among penguins
nesting and molting on the continent itself. Sunset

blazed just as the ship moved so far from Ushuaia
she could barely discern the Tierra del Fuego town
becoming a silvery blur, lights twinkling on while
land masses the Russian captain steered through
shimmered in delicate peach tints across snow,
mystifying her and nearly everyone else until
a scientist explained the ethereal hues were algae.
"Albatross!" a crew mate cried. She followed

his finger aiming at the white surprise of her first
albatross which she had longed to see ever since
she was fourteen and read Coleridge's tragic
"Rime of the Ancient Mariner." But this bird
with its immense span of cloud-dark wings
would fly through a twilight of sky an orange fire
over water mirroring those flames in multiple waves,
carrying her spirit on its alive free soaring.

After that evening, ship moved mutely on
to where sun often was a hint behind mist,
an elusive star in fog slashed by freezing rains
and winds that made her take sea sickness pills
then crawl into her cabin's tiny bed where she
could draw curtains like albatross wings and dream
of roving again where life was steady beneath her feet.
But when calmer weather came, the crew took the curious

on zodiac boats near where mother whales and calves
hung shadow-like in bay water and seals lolled about
on ice floes of blues for which no poet had ever conjured
names, a fairy world of glaciers in variations of aquamarine,
glints of original starlight flashing a translucent code
of tongueless beauty to the one who knew other Blues
back in the country where poets are scorned,
so close her hand could almost touch its glow.

Comunidad Indigena Andrés Licán, Andes, Chile

Headed for another "middle of nowhere" I cannot
    imagine – John driving us higher and wilder in Andes,

paradise of blackberries hanging bunched
    and low by dirt road, siren call to pick

the plumpest blackberries in Chile,
    so near I can reach arm and hand

through open window to pluck those berries
    reminding me of home. Only I spot wasps

clustered around the fermenting fruit,
    striped yellow drunks bellied up to our lunch.

Despite John's theory that we might still do our gathering
    due to the insects' buzzing stupor, I don't wish to risk

being stung by hundreds of wasps hundreds of kilometers
    from any hospital. So John drives on, a river sparkles below,

Subaru wheels kick up transient whirlwinds
    of ale brown dust. Makes me thirsty, the fast waters,

the memory of ale, and those berries evoking
    my brother Danny's blackberry wine and happy times.

First tinges of autumn, March grass slightly gold,
     a cooling in the blue Andean air, tin roofed shacks

on mountainsides and where earth greets the river.
     A family appears like an ancient dream, man with guitar,

a wife, daughters, little boy. John stops the car, *"Buenos días!"* –
     never shy as I am, not one to worry about the shyness of others,

while my reserve understands these are Indians
     traditionally polite and smiling as I am smiling

until we are congregating with them on the road.
     "It is my son's fourth birthday," the father explains,

"we are walking home from celebrating at the church."
     John knows Spanish unlike me who only comprehends

the light around people's bodies, why their eyes glow,
     what their way of walking says like a wordless song.

I understand the colors they chose to wear, this family
     that flames like a flower garden where the true language

isn't *Español* or indigenous words but grins, giggles, laughter –
     illuminations of wonderment in all our faces. How can I say

You remind me of my family six decades ago in our mountains,
     of when we were poor and still went to church and I was innocent,

a watchful Indian girl long before all the years at university,
     of metamorphosis into a creature called educated and sophisticated?

We decide to take photographs of each other with our cell phones.
    Sí, even in the Andes people have cellies, and beautiful we pose

and promise to write via Facebook. Beloved family –
    now a photographic bouquet of human flowers whose spirit

I shall fly home to New York. Waving *"adiós,"* John drives on
    past pebble path to your small farm in these Andes that break

my heart with an old unspeakable beauty, far beyond the sign
    of faded red letters someone's hand once proudly painted,

COMUNIDAD INDIGENA ANDRE LICAN.
PTE BASA CHICO.

One February Night of Sleeping with Sea Lions

First time we spotted sea lions south of Caleta Olivia, we edged
near as we could to them until John dropped on all fours, lifting
head up in Argentinian sun that way the bulls raised their heads
in a dark leonine magnificence surveying females and pups
on golden sand bordering Atlantic, starry sparkles pirouetting
across azure waves the great pinnipeds dove in and out of –
and I wishing I could swim with the pod for the February air
was so torrid. But we had seen signs warning us to keep
our distance and I hung back while wondering if a cow
would drag herself over to my damn fool roving companion
and try to mate with him. Meanwhile, a thick-necked male
roared sea-lion style in John's direction until he raced laughing
back to me, sand flying off long bare legs and arms.

Second time we saw the sea lions was on our return
from Ushuaia and Antarctica, tired as fuck after wending
north over Patagonia steppe, past red sky sunset on to full
moon rising through strands of smoky clouds like remnants
of hope. When we spotted the beach, John parked on cliff
overlooking the sea lions' silhouettes where waves surged
to shore. Rolling down windows, we watched moonlit bodies
as if teenagers once more at a drive-in movie, giggling
at their cacophony of sounds like belches, farts and baas.
Eyes closing, I dreamed of my first night in a car with John,
girl he still calls "the hot chick" straddling him on front seat,
1970 moon rays grazing amazed face, first time, flinging
his head back the way sea lions do. How could we have known
we'd come together all the way to Tierra del Fuego?

The Pack Dogs of Uspallata, Argentina

After crossing *El Paso de Internacional Los Libertadores*, high
Andes border pass switch-backing from Chile to Argentina,
we meandered to Uspallata, pulling into a red-trimmed restaurant's
parking lot to study Google maps for roads we might wish to take
deeper inland. Malbec vineyards were calling to me, scent of
Mendoza grapes a taste of paradise, poets dancing the tango
with overflowing wine bottles glinting in South American sun.
My head bowed to maps, at first I didn't see the dogs –
only heard them through rolled down windows, strident barks
a noose tightening around desperate yelps conjuring up the time
a man sped his snowmobile into my German Shepherd pup,
slashing her right leg, bone springing out into the frigid air,
blood color of garnets gushing to snowy ground. One never
forgets such howls of pain, nor the panic of how to save
a beautiful animal. I raised my head to bring face and eyes
to gaze at six mongrels, three black, three dirty brown, nipping
and biting a soft tawny dog splayed on her back, lunging at
her exposed underside while her legs jerked helplessly.
Over and over her canine screams echoed those of my puppy,
the pack bearing down on her. "Stop it, stop it, you bastards!!"
I let loose my own screams but the mutts wouldn't listen.
I opened my door and slammed it shut, opened it, slammed it,
shrieking at what I had always hated, the animal or human
who joins the pack or mob. I glimpsed a hole in the bitch's
soft pink belly, for bitch she was to them, their bared teeth
plunging in to rip the dark hole larger. "Stop!" I yelped,
shaking in rage and fear, for I didn't dare leave the car

to kick away the snarling dogs who might leap on me and rip
open my belly. Had I a gun I would have shot each attacker
then carried the traumatized female in my trembling arms
to where her wounds could be healed. Why did people
walk by as if nothing was happening? I remembered times
when males in a pack terrified me, bold in their bonding,
primed to slap, punch, kick, rape, pumped up on each other's
testosterone mixing with macho sweat. Even educated men,
claiming they weren't like the rest, would rip females apart
with sarcasm or swaggering wit pretending to be civilized.
"Nothing you can do about those dogs," my mate sped away,
gunning for the wineries of Mendoza.

Pampas Flamingo

Even home again in Catskills, that hot day
of driving countless kilometers across the pampas
of an Argentina January flashes back to me

where summer solstice now approaches
and the trees' greens darken and breezes make
whispers of their leaves sheltering newborn birds

and late spring fawns. Abundant the wildness
in these mountains, let us give thanks,
for I have traveled in a land where nearly

every wild creature was slaughtered, every
free being – Indian, mammal, butterfly, bird –
disappeared by the *estancias* of the rich,

their branded cows destined for *parrilla* barbecues
and the bellies of the greatest meat eaters
who ever had a taste for fat and blood.

Even here in these northern mountains
I sometimes shudder at the unspeakable absence
called pampas where I wanted to scream

from weariness, boredom, and primordial fear.
Except that one afternoon of staring out
the car's passenger window at sky

so bright its blue blanched to white –
when a flamingo appeared, brave blaze
of coral feathers tinged by deeper flames

migrating in the fierce air, legs long stems
and it a stray elegant flower, a rose resistance
startling me into a moment's delight

of chanting "Flamingo, flamingo!"
O sun-singed day painted anew
by the pink phoenix of the pampas.

Etta Place, Our Lady of Maybes

(for Steve of the Manor)

That January day John and I made a pilgrimage to the cabin
where you, Etta, and the Sundance Kid (your lover),
and Butch Cassidy (perhaps another lover) "played
respectable" for four years after escaping the law
growing too lawful back in the States, I was reminded
of the red shrines to Gauchito Gil, "saint" of Patagonia,
Robin Hood of Argentina, one to whom the Indians bring
scarlet gifts and prayers. Even in this 21st century
a challenge to find where you and your two sweet talkers
bought a ranch in a vastness of rock and raptors plunging
countless kilometers down to Tierra del Fuego's Ushuaia
perched above Beagle Channel's siren song waters.

No road signs hinted at where your cabin still stood,
just as there blaze no definitive signs pointing to your
birth name that metamorphosed into several names,
just as there exist no stories snaking to some simple truth
tamer people seek behind your legend, Etta, Ethel, Ann, etc.
Maybe you worked in a brothel, maybe as a schoolteacher,
maybe eventually you rejoined Sundance in North America
and lived together until he died in 1946 Wyoming.
Out there on the steppe several miles from Cholila,
close enough to the Andean border to escape into Chile,
mystery prevails over gossip and rumors.

John and I kept asking the way until a gaucho from his
stallion showed us a pebbly road with grass in its middle.
In the fierce summer heat of South America's upside
down world we hiked to where you lay low and grew bored,
until you and your darlings pulled off a brilliant bank robbery
in Río Gallegos. Who would have suspected this of the pretty
red haired, green-eyed lady who attended Patagonian soirees
in long silken dresses with a silken tongue to match? Yet
the gossips hissed you cut off your hair, often dressed in pants,
could shoot as sharp as Butch and Sundance on a horse
galloping madly as Patagonian winds. It was a wig your wore
for charming purposes while speaking a dulcet *Español*.

Hollywood titled their movie about you three young people
"Butch Cassidy and the Sundance Kid," no mention of you
who they depicted as a virginal teacher falling for a "wild guy,"
male literary theme no doubt going back to the caves
and ancient nights when we learned to make stories and fires.
No hint that even docile men, not just rebels, can be ignited
by women ablaze like the Big Bang's first stardust.
Six thousand miles from Catskills I call home, Etta,
I dawdled with John down that road more like path
where you strode, sunned by your cabin door, lazed
within on an old wooden chair where light streamed through
windows no longer shuttered against Pinkertons, encircled
by trees and grasses sloping to a creek and quick way out.

You did it, Etta, you did it, my poet's heart expanded
to a universe of chant, of shout. How many women
had told me after my poetry readings that they had once
yearned to be writers? How many women trembled
that my poetry spoke what they were never brave enough

to howl, their love, their sorrow, their loss, their rage?
How many dead dreams have women and men whispered
into my ear as if it were the hole in the tree for telling secrets?
And if I could weave further magic, I would create
other scarlet shrines in Patagonia and North America,
candlelit stops for you, Etta, your name for eternity
Our Lady of Maybes, elusive free one with hair of fire.

Red Road of Yellow
Butterflies, Argentina

There are things I try not to mention in this country,
for instance the tortured and *los desaparecidos* –
not that I speak *Español* except as a child lilts new words.

And it is as a child I ride with John through
this northern province bordering Brazil and Paraguay,
where Iguazú Falls brings people from many lands

together, voices mingling in exclamations
of wonder, tangos of awe danced to the soft
high pitch of adults speaking to the innocent.

Here is a place for being childlike again,
in this magical time between Christmas
and New Year, on this red dirt road John drives

down the day after we leave the giant cascades
circled by jungle emerald as first dreams, trails
bordered by flowers we have no names for –

here that place before we knew the word "beauty"
or braved a first kiss, bouncing through mud puddles
until Subaru windshield and all the rest

is splattered. We have been in this land
long enough to laugh, "Hey, it's Argentina!"
Then the yellow butterflies appear,

thousands flashing in insect-buzzing sunlight –
and, fewer in number, azure ones like miniature mirrors
of two Blue Morphos who surprised us at Iguazú,

iridescent above, camouflage below.
A rare orange butterfly flames into the car,
alighting on my arm in what feels like kinship,

and I walk out among the butterflies,
photographing and filming them in the hope I may
transport my wonder to the people back home

in winter's snows and deepening freeze,
transmit that sensation of wings brushing my skin
with the tiniest of feathers, until my senses

take flight and I dare to be simply happy, a whirl
of pure yellow, my favorite childhood color.
Except we old ones remember about paradise,

sí, I am bitten by flies and unseen things
and John hears "something funny," our third flat tire
in Argentina we soon learn, only this high noon

on a red jungle road far from any *gomeria*.
He kneels in the dirt, turns blood-red from it,
fixing the flat while fear stings my cheek in fire-like air,

for here Guarani Indians were disappeared
and the ones who lived learned to hide how they flew
with butterflies the same as my people did.

Sisterhood in Sucre, Bolivia

Before making it to Sucre, John drove us up to Altiplano
which promised geysers somewhere, high Bolivian plain
stretching for a gamble of endless kilometers, desolate
stretches of dirt, rock, occasional mountains, road maybe,
and surprise salt flats reflecting flocks of flamingos,
azure water turned rose by elegant bird bodies. Stopping
to watch them dip long curved beaks into the gift
of water in a stark land, we marveled over their thin stems
of legs making them appear like many mirages of wildflowers
atop the stems – and if we were lucky an entire flock would
suddenly fly, transforming midday into sunset or sunrise, we had
our pick. Our eyes changed, too, adapting to a different part
of earth and sky, acquiring the gaze of Pachamama country.

Before almost not making it to Sucre, we found what
turned out to be fumaroles after banging over rocks, into dips,
sometimes losing track of what passed as road, other times
losing sight of any tracks in the desert dirt. Finally we spotted
smoke rising up from what looked like nowhere, a scattering
of smelly fumaroles at twilight when we had no choice but
to sleep out in our dusty Subaru in freezing altiplano night.
We rustled up a picnic of peanut butter and strawberry preserves
on crackers, I swigged back some wine, and we shimmied
inside sleeping bags, watching smoke too close for my taste
while full moon rose over nearby mountain. I woke at ten,
"Jack Frost" blurring car windows, shaking John awake,
screaming the winds were blowing sulfurous smoke
all around us, we could die. He drove to a spot outside

the eerie dance of smoke, and after a night of nervous sleep
we woke before dawn and watched the sun rise, stumbling out
to greet it and pee and wander shivering around fumaroles hissing
the spirit of that isolated place desolate and beautiful all at once.
And then we ventured out on another region of the altiplano,
saw a few vehicles with guides to show less crazy tourists
sunrise above fumaroles, until there were no human beings,
just frail full moon sinking towards mountain blood red
against cloudless sky. If we failed to find our way out
we could meet death by day's heat or night's desert freeze.
If the car broke down we might not be found in time.
Eventually, we followed a dry stream bed leading
to tracks entering into what approximated a road,
headed for Sucre and some old colonial hotel
to make up for subjecting our aging bones to sleeping
on the front seat of Subaru whose muffler was now
deafening loud with shocks shot and steering wheel

starting to lock. In Sucre, John took the car to a mechanic
and when it was ready we walked there together because
the man and his family wanted to meet the *poetissa*
from *Estados Unidos*. They dragged out chairs for us
on patio between adobe walls and offered us Coca Cola,
invited us to lunch. Women cooking, men tinkering
with cars, children playing tag – and I asking the mothers
if they could tell me what life was like for my Bolivian sisters
since I had seen *mucho* feminist graffiti and murals of rage
against *machismo* on countless stairways, walls and gates .
No decent birth control, they said, *no abortion rights, girls*
barely in their teens having babies while their boyfriends
often ran away and the girls sometimes left their infants
in the streets because they were too poor to keep them.

128

John offered to take photographs of us new *amigas* –
we *hermanas* draping arms around each other, flashing
peace symbols then laughingly waving middle fingers
like defiant flags in that land where it is too easy to die.

To the Children of South America Who Dream of Coming to *los Estados Unidos*

To the children of South America I met after I was diagnosed
with breast cancer, had surgery, then radiation treatments,
to you I encountered when my roving companion and I flew
to Chile, only a few months since the last radiation beams
pierced my body and I wondered if I could roam as I once had,
still sad, saddled with fatigue, aching in my left breast now
nestled differently near my heart – to you I give that heart
because you reminded me of how I had big dreams when still
a small mountain girl of the "part Indian" kind, helped me recall
no matter how poor, hurt, afraid, and knocked down we are
the dreaming is free and maybe we can keep it.

To the Chilean children in a one room schoolhouse far out
on isolated dirt road – gratitude. To you smiling at us old
North Americans who offered to be Monday's English lesson,
you who amazed us with a Mapuche Indian song about the life
of a shaman, so perfect when I was Mohawk, I want you to know
that since that morning my heart beats to your drum, flute,
and passionate singing. To the girl who gushed to us when
she learned we were from Nueva York, "I want to fly north
to visit the Empire State building and ride its elevator to the top,"
I am glad I could say I once had the same dream and finally
rode to the top, why I believed your dream would also come true.
To you students who painted such vivid pictures hanging on
the humble walls, your art moved me more than museum paintings.

To the children of Bolivia, sons and daughters in a land
sixty percent Indian with an Aymara Indian President, to you
in your numerous poverties on the altiplano, in the high Andes,
in dusty pueblos and cities with rebars shooting up from the never
finished adobe houses and dog shit and trash on the streets and
dumped along roads knifing across your third world country's
surreal beauty – gratitude. To the little sister and brother
John brought to our car to meet me while their parents rustled
up gas for us in a border town, know your faces mirrored mine
when I was an unsmiling child. Boy of sweet sad searing eyes,
may your desire to come to our country be fulfilled as much
as my wish to come to yours. May you bring your sister.

To the street boys of Santa Cruz de la Sierra, and Susana
who is helping you find a better life – gratitude. You made me
know that a spirit glows in everyone because despite your lives
branded by tragedies, you talked and smiled and laughed that night
John made everyone tacos and I contributed Christmas cookies
and Ferrero Rocher chocolates for dessert, poets' cuisine. I won't
forget you understood my poem about long Indian hair on the card
I gave to each of you, will always be touched by your gifts to us.
If only I could fly you here, show you the white peacock feather
and matchbox cars now unique muses safe in my study. Lastly,
to the child beggars of Bolivia and Peru, your upturned hands
countless as the stars, *Indios* similar to the desperadoes seeking
exile at the U.S./Mexico border – gratitude. Thanks to you,
every dawn I hold out my own upturned hands asking for change.

Tambopata National Reserve, Peru

Boat of open sides run by Indian guides carried us
to the Refugio Amazonas Lodge, three hours on Peru's
Tambopata River squeezed in among other tourists
seeking "the rainforest experience." Sun and cloud
fought for dominance in sky the roof sheltered us from,
we hoped a jaguar would appear at jungle edge
But no sacred cat came, jaguars invisible the same
as most indigenous people in that Reserve a shadowy
tangle of mysteries like two vast alien wings sprung
from muddy *agua* churned up by the rainy season
just beginning. Only a capybara reminding me
of our Catskill woodchucks showed up on shore,
rolling in soft mud, and further on a caiman's
knobby black snout and green gold eyes rose above
the river then sank noiselessly back down, its merciless
stare leaving behind a chill of fear even in jungle heat.
At last we reached the Refugio's landing, traipsed
on a narrow path to welcoming lodge where we had
to shed our shoes before ascending wide wooden steps
to great communal rooms for conversing, drinking
and dining. I ordered a pisco sour straightaway,
sipping paradise at the bar whose giant mirror reflected
Blue Morphos flapping wings flashing like neon beyond
the impressive architecture that held no glass windows
only extravagant openings to help immerse us in jungle,
a delirium of butterflies evoking ancestors and ancestresses
all the way back to first mother in Africa, and further to
Neanderthals and Denisovans, their DNA in my blood rivers,

my transient life floating up the dreams of countless migrations
bringing my lover and me to Peru. But despite being old,
camouflaged gray beneath folded wings like the Blue Morpho's
when closed, that twilight my heart metamorphosed into a *refugio*
of butterflies, a flight of drunk blue fires.

The Way to Rainbow Mountain

We saved the new year for finding our way
to Peru's Rainbow Mountain – January 9th,
my roving companion John's 69th birthday.
What better celebration than to seek that peak
of many colors concealed until four years ago,
climate change freeing the mountain's
thick poncho of ice. Ever since I first saw
a picture of Vinicunca, "seven colored mountain,"
I dreamed in its direction, my heart beating
to whatever awaited me in Incan Andes, soul

frozen by the Ice Age of *los Estados Unidos locos*,
by all the hate and crazy and then breast cancer
that hit two Mays ago. *Sí*, I dreamed of ascending
to Rainbow Mountain and maybe thaw to the woman
of color I once was. Chile, Argentina, Bolivia,
lastly Peru –wandering through desert, altiplano,
along ocean and over cloud-touching passes
down into pueblos and cities looking bombed out
except in the *turista* areas, and John on his birthday
driving us ever higher on road winding

to the base camp of his birthday gift,
steep drops from crumbling dirt edges
reminding us why people pray to whatever gods
or goddesses they hope exist. How close we came
to plummeting off cliffs where vultures keep watch.
Then we made it to the trail's beginning,
hail pelting down, mists like shape-shifters

swirling through a vast valley and snaking around
mountainsides. Two Indian guides led us up

on their horses, I in three layers of clothes
marveling at my guide seemingly gliding
in bare feet and sandals through hail stones,
patches of snow, puddles and streams. When
my mare, gentle and reddish brown, stopped,
the guide talked low and kind to her until we
continued on. John's horse, a stallion, whinnied
and pranced sometimes while I patted my mare
on her neck as softly as the guide spoke. We had to
disembark and trudge up the final vertical of path.

Despite the Diamox I took, I could barely
breathe, feared I might have to crawl to reach
that place I needed to go. John grabbed
my hand, gripped it tight and helped pull me
to the mountaintop facing Rainbow Mountain,
the *mirador*, for no human was allowed to step on
the mineral-made sacred rainbow. I knelt
by stone wall, refuge from winds 16000 feet high,
gazed as llamas, alpacas, vicuñas, and descendants
of Incas gazed in their ur-language of silence.

"O beautiful holy Rainbow Mountain, we greet you
and we thank you." And your "*De nada*," Mountain?
Sun parting clouds, just as we met an indigenous family
celebrating their matriarch's 60th birthday, everyone
in traditional clothes, grandmother vivid like the gift
of the rainbows. "Happy Birthday, *Feliz Cumpleaños!*"
We smiled, talked, laughed, took photographs
of each other, of our two Americas coming together,
warming me back to a woman of color.

Bio

Susan Deer Cloud, a mixed lineage Catskill Indian, is an alumna of Goddard College (MFA) and Binghamton University (B.A. and M.A.). She has taught Creative Writing, Rhetoric and Literature at Binghamton University and Broome Community College. In April 2013 she returned to her "heart country" Catskills to dwell once more with foxes, deer, black bears, rainbow trout, bald eagles, and the ghosts of panthers and ancestors. She now lives as a full-time mountain woman, dreamer and writer in between roaming on Turtle Island and in other lands.

Deer Cloud is the recipient of various awards and fellowships, including an Elizabeth George Foundation Grant, a National Endowment for the Arts Literature Fellowship, two New York State Foundation for the Arts Fellowships, and a Chenango County Council for the Arts Individual Artist's Grant. Some of her books are *Before Language* and *Hunger Moon* (Shabda Press); *Fox Mountain, The Last Ceremony* and *Car Stealer* (FootHills Publishing); and *Braiding Starlight* (Split Oak Press). Her poems, stories and essays have been published in anthologies and journals too numerous to name.

In order to get out "the voices of the voiceless," the poet has edited three published anthologies: multicultural *Confluence* and Native American anthologies *I Was Indian (Before Being Indian Was Cool), Volumes I & II;* the 2008 Spring Issue of *Yellow Medicine Review, a Journal of Indigenous Literature, Art & Thought*; and the Re-Matriation Chapbook Series of Indigenous Poetry. She is a member of the international travel/peace organization SERVAS, Poets & Writers, and Associated Writing Programs (AWP). She has served on panels at writers' conferences and given myriad poetry readings at colleges, cultural centers, coffee houses, and other venues.

Deer Cloud has spent the past few years roving with her wanderlust companion, John Gunther, in the far north of Canada's Maritime Provinces and in South America (Chile, Argentina, Bolivia and Peru). After being diagnosed with breast cancer in May 2017, more than ever this poet is immersed in an open ended physical journey mated to a spirit quest for whatever original stardust-light draws us to each other in the most creative, tender, and enraptured ways.

www.ingramcontent.com/pod-product-compliance
Lightning Source LLC
Chambersburg PA
CBHW022135080426
42734CB00006B/367